ENGLAND, INDIA, AND AFGHANISTAN

ENGLAND, INDIA, AND AFGHANISTAN

AN ESSAY UPON

THE RELATIONS, PAST AND FUTURE,
BETWEEN AFGHANISTAN AND THE
BRITISH EMPIRE IN INDIA

THE LE BAS PRIZE ESSAY, 1902

BY

FRANK NOYCE, B.A.,

SCHOLAR OF ST CATHARINE'S COLLEGE

LONDON
C. J. CLAY AND SONS
CAMBRIDGE UNIVERSITY PRESS WAREHOUSE
AVE MARIA LANE.

1902

CAMBRIDGE UNIVERSITY PRESS
Cambridge, New York, Melbourne, Madrid, Cape Town,
Singapore, São Paulo, Delhi, Mexico City

Cambridge University Press
The Edinburgh Building, Cambridge CB2 8RU, UK

Published in the United States of America by Cambridge University Press, New York

www.cambridge.org
Information on this title: www.cambridge.org/9781107610903

First published 1902
First paperback edition 2013

A catalogue record for this publication is available from the British Library

ISBN 978-1-107-61090-3 Paperback

TO THE

REV. E. R. BERNARD,
CHANCELLOR OF SALISBURY CATHEDRAL,

IN GRATEFUL REMEMBRANCE

OF MUCH KINDNESS.

CONTENTS.

PREFACE.

"No writer," as Lord Curzon has well said, "should approach the Central Asian question without a consciousness of its magnitude, or venture to decide it without long previous study." For that study he will find material ample, but often extremely unsatisfactory, which divides itself roughly into three great divisions.

In the first place there are the Government Blue Books, the ultimate resort of historians of every shade of opinion, which, whilst for the later years they form a more or less impartial, though by no means complete, record of events, are not for the earlier ones above a suspicion of being tampered with to suit the ends of policy[1].

Secondly, we get the work of the historians of the Afghan wars. Much of this, and especially of the more recent part of it, is highly controversial in character, for unfortunately quite early in its history the Afghan question became one of party

[1] *e.g.* Burnes' correspondence with Lord Auckland.

politics, and politicians are not always capable of
judging persons or policies upon their merits alone.
The First Afghan War is sufficiently distant for
historians to agree in great measure as to its
wisdom, but though twenty years have elapsed
since its close, the storm of party bitterness aroused
by the events which brought about the war of 1878
has not even yet died away sufficiently to enable
that war to be viewed dispassionately, and for the
conclusions regarding it to be unanimous.

Finally, we have the work of those who have
assisted in subordinate capacities in making Afghan
and Indian history—namely, Indian frontier officials and Afghan boundary commissioners. In
this there is—perhaps of necessity—a refreshing
lack of controversy. The writers have usually
contented themselves with little more than a bare
recital of facts, leaving the reader to draw his own
conclusions. As to the policy which has sent them
forth to do what they have done they are silent.
Their work has however one great drawback, lack
of perspective. One who is engaged in a particular sphere of work is apt to lose sight of perspective and to regard his own field of energy as
the all-important one. The fact that they have
been unable to estimate their work as but a small
factor in a great problem detracts greatly from the
value of much that has been written concerning

the Indian frontier by those who have seen active service upon it.

These are the three great sources of information concerning the Afghan question. The mass of literature which has been written upon it in newspapers and reviews, when of any importance at all, will generally be found to rank under, or be derived from, one or other of these heads.

It is almost impossible to write anything original concerning the Afghan question without studying it for years at first hand. Whatever originality this essay may claim lies in the fact that the writer has endeavoured to form his own opinions unbiassed by party considerations after giving due weight to those of others. This has been especially the case with regard to the Second Afghan War, in dealing with which he has attempted to divide the responsibility more equally, if not more justly, than it is usually divided.

The easiest part of the task of the writer upon Afghanistan lies in the consideration of the future, for it is no difficult matter to prophesy. The difficulty lies in prophesying correctly, for the Eastern question is capable of such kaleidoscopic changes that many eventualities have to be considered. These as far as possible have been taken into account in dealing with the future relations of India and Afghanistan.

A list of the books, of very varying degrees of utility, which have been consulted, will be found at the end of the volume. Specific obligations to them, to the Government Blue Books, and to articles in reviews and newspapers too numerous to be mentioned in detail, have been acknowledged in the notes.

I have to thank the adjudicators, Sir R. K. Wilson, Bart., and Mr G. P. Moriarty, for permission to alter the essay before publication and for many valuable suggestions. To Mr Moriarty especially I am indebted for much help in the rectification of omissions. My thanks are also due to my friend, the Rev. J. N. Figgis, for his kindness in correcting the proof-sheets.

FRANK NOYCE.

St Catharine's College,
August 16, 1902.

CHAPTER I.

INTRODUCTORY.

Comparison between India and Italy, Afghanistan and Savoy.—
Position of Afghanistan with reference to the Central Asian
Question.—Nature of the Russian advance in Central Asia.—
British policy in the past.

GEOGRAPHERS and historians are notoriously fond
of parallels. None has had a greater attraction
for them than that between the three southern
European and Asiatic peninsulas. And certainly
in the case of the midmost of these, India and
Italy, many striking points of resemblance both
in geography and history can be found. The
southern half of each peninsula has always been
inhabited by unwarlike and peace-loving peoples
at the mercy of the nation which dominated the
northern or continental portion. But its retention
has usually proved a matter of some difficulty, if
the dominant nation did not at the same time
possess a certain command of the sea, to attacks
from which Naples and Madras have always been
singularly open.

Further, the fertile plains of Bengal and Lombardy have from time immemorial been at the mercy of invaders from the west. Owing to the physical configuration of India and Italy, the danger of invasion from the north and east has always been small compared with that from the west, and in consequence, the ruler of the state which commands the routes from the west has generally had an importance out of all proportion to the wealth or population of his kingdom. Sir Alfred Lyall has advanced an interesting and instructive comparison between the Afghanistan of to-day and the Armenia of the first and second centuries of our era. But in pursuance of our comparison between India and Italy, another striking historical parallel can be found, namely, between Afghanistan and Savoy in the seventeenth and eighteenth centuries. Afghanistan is much more the Savoy of Asia than the Switzerland, and its position between England and Russia is very much like that of Savoy between France and Austria in 1700. But parallels, however close, are only useful up to a certain point, and, if pushed too far, are apt to become dangerously misleading. It is not in the least probable that Abdur Rahman, though not a whit behind Victor Amadeus in ability and statecraft, and though his alliance was a matter of as much importance to England or Russia as was that of the ruler of Savoy to France or Austria, has laid a foundation upon which Afghanistan will be able to absorb India as did Savoy the rest of Italy. Suffice it to say that, at the present time, no country in the world owes its importance less to its wealth, population, and resources, and more to its geographical position than does Afghanistan. Its continued existence as an independent state is due to that alone. And therefore, before proceeding to discuss the past relations of Afghanistan and the British Empire in detail, it may be well at the outset to endeavour to obtain a clear view of the position of Afghanistan in relation to the Central Asian problem. The determining factor of the British dealings with regard to it has never been any desire to possess it for its own sake. Intrinsically, it is worth nothing, but as a magnificent natural outwork for the defence of the Indian Empire it could scarcely be equalled, and its value as such has been fully recognized by British statesmen since the commencement of their rule in India. It has never been their practice to make the sphere of British influence coincide with the frontier of the territory over which the British Government exercises administrative jurisdiction. Perhaps as a consequence of insular traditions, they have always been mistrustful of a frontier between

the British dominion in India and the dominion of
any rival power, such as that between France and
Germany. As a belt of sea is impossible, they
have always preferred a zone of territory over
which political influence can be exercised without
at the same time heavy governmental responsibilities being incurred. This zone of territory,
consisting of states of varying degrees of independence, has been established on the eastern and
western sides of the British Empire in India, but
that on the western side has always been infinitely
the more important, since the dangers of invasion
from that side have always been much the greater.
For many years Oudh occupied the uncomfortable
position of a barrier state, but, as the Empire increased towards the limits fixed by nature in the
Himalaya mountains and their offshoots, Oudh was
absorbed and a new outer line of defence became
necessary. By this time the character of the
possible invaders of India had changed also. No
longer was it likely that it would ever again be
at the mercy of a horde of undisciplined and
barbarous warriors. Its antagonists in the future
would be civilized nations of undoubted military
strength. France was the first European power
which threatened the safety of India, but its place
was very soon taken by Russia. In the future it may
be Russia, with France playing a secondary part.

The nature of the Russian advance in Central Asia, which has almost since their commencement been the determining factor in British relations with Afghanistan, has been much misunderstood and its purposes often grossly exaggerated. It is a great mistake to regard it as altogether the outcome of a Machiavellian policy, fixed and unswerving, which has India and India alone as its final destination. The Russian system of government has its drawbacks as well as the English, and there is ample room for inconsistency in the former as well as in the latter. The disadvantages of the English system of party government have, as we shall see later, been even more conspicuous in Afghanistan than elsewhere, but the Russian *régime* also has defects, which, though not perhaps so noticeable, are yet quite as far-reaching. Russian diplomacy has been much overrated and is often as shortsighted as it is unscrupulous. This is the natural outcome of a method of government which has neither united counsel nor plan of action. Everything depends upon an individual initiative, which is tempered only by the personal authority of the Czar, and the result of this is bound to be weakness and disagreement[1]. Such has been frequently the case in Central Asia, and Russian history contains one or two disasters

[1] Curzon, *Russia in Central Asia*, p. 316.

worthy to rank with our first and greatest failure
in Afghanistan—notably Perovski's expedition to
Khiva in 1839, which in point of time almost
coincided with it. At the same time Russian
ministers know how to turn to account even this
source of weakness. In the hands of strong politicians it may even become a source of strength.
For it enables them to disavow the actions of
subordinates when unsuccessful, or when the storm
aroused by them is out of proportion to the advantage gained, and to utilise them to the full
whenever possible. But as a consequence, the
Russian advance in Central Asia has not been as
undeviating as is usually supposed. It has been
largely due to force of circumstances, and at times
the policy which has been pursued has been one
of waiting upon events. Pledges have been given
that it should not proceed beyond a certain point,
and those pledges have been broken, as might have
been confidently predicted by an acute observer at
the time. For a strong and civilized nation, which
has as neighbours weak and barbarous states, will
inevitably end by absorbing those states. No
blame attaches to Russia for this. It has been
for the advantage of civilization generally, and
Great Britain is the last nation which can justly
complain, as its own conduct has been similar on
very many occasions. The process has been going

on for the last half century in South Africa, and
to take instances nearer the subject, our attitude
towards Burmah, Sind, and the Punjab differs very
little from that of Russia towards Khiva, Bokhara,
and Trans-Caspia generally. As Lord Lawrence
said in 1868, we have not the right openly to
question or impede the Russian advance so long
as it is not clearly directed against our interests[1].
But that it is a serious menace to England, and
that it may in the future gravely affect our interests
in India cannot be denied. Great Britain in India
is a continental power, a fact too often overlooked
by British statesmen. Whilst British and Russian
interests may conflict in many parts of the world,
in China, Persia, or Turkey, the borderland of India
is the only spot where the two nations can meet in
the guise of rival military powers. And it is this
fact which renders our relations with Afghanistan
so important and intricate a question. The necessity of some measures, if not to check the Russian
advance, at any rate to fortify India against it,
was early recognized by British statesmen, but
unfortunately, almost equally early, there arose
serious differences as to the proper measures to
be taken. India has suffered much with regard to
its foreign policy, both from the disadvantages of
party government, and from its dual government—

[1] *Afghan Blue Book* (1), 1878, p. 61.

a Secretary of State at home and a Governor-General at Calcutta. In no part of its foreign relations has this been more clearly apparent than in those with Afghanistan. Almost at the outset of its history—at any rate from the great disaster of 1842 onwards—the Afghan question became a party one. The inevitable result was that during the greater part of the last century, instead of a settled line of policy, we get an alternation backwards and forwards, a policy of ill-timed and ill-considered advances followed by one of mis-interpreted defeats. Only in the last two decades of the nineteenth century was there evolved out of the chaos of the Second Afghan War a plan of action to which both political parties could give their allegiance, a plan which partook of the nature of a compromise between the extremes on which each had suffered shipwreck, masterly inactivity and meddling interference.

CHAPTER II.

FROM EARLY TIMES TO THE END OF THE FIRST AFGHAN WAR (1842).

Early Afghan History.—The invasions of India by Nadir and Ahmad Shah.—Effect of the Battle of Panipat.—Zaman Shah.—Sir John Shore's minute upon Afghan affairs.—Treaty with Persia.—Anarchy in Afghanistan.—Expulsion of Shah Shuja by Dost Mahomed.—Failure of Dost Mahomed's appeal to Lord Auckland.—Arrival of a Russian envoy at Kabul.—Lord Auckland's Afghan policy.—Action of the Home Government.—The Tripartite Treaty.—The First Afghan War.—Effect of the British failure upon Afghan and British relations.

IT is obviously impossible, without transforming a brief essay on the relations of Great Britain with Afghanistan in the past into an epitome of the historical facts to be found in the ordinary text-books of Indian history, to do more than touch upon the chief events of Afghan history in so far as they illustrate the policy which has been pursued towards that unhappy country. It is equally impossible and almost equally undesirable, with regard to a matter on which so much has been written by statesmen and officials of every grade of ability and experience, to comment upon any views other than those of men whose words have brought about action.

Afghan history is small and characteristically Oriental. It is practically bound up with the history of the English in India, for Afghanistan as a separate state is quite a modern growth, and sprang into existence almost at the same time as the British dominion in the East. A century and a half ago Afghanistan was nominally an outlying province of the Moghul Empire. The Western Afghans had overrun Persia, whilst the eastern half was in the hands of a number of small semi-independent tribes. Nadir Shah freed Persia from the Afghans, whom he employed to assist him in his Indian invasions, and reannexed Kandahar to Persia. He was succeeded by Ahmad Shah, an Afghan, who was crowned king at Ahmad Shahr, the modern Kandahar, which he made the capital of his dominions. This prince proved an even more terrible scourge to India than his predecessor. The great battle fought between his forces and the Mahrattas on the historic field of Panipat in 1761 exercised a far-reaching though indirect influence upon the fortunes of the British in India. For the crushing defeat of the Mahrattas put an end to the pretensions of the only native power, which, by reason of its organization and cohesion, had any prospect of reducing India under one rule. Had the Mahrattas been successful at Panipat, the Moghul Empire would have received another lease of life with the Peishwa as Mayor of the Palace, and that at a time when the British, owing to the weakness of their own position, could not have interfered. The accession to the Mahratta power thus brought about would have made them exceedingly difficult to dislodge later. As it was, however, the Mahrattas never really recovered from the blow they sustained at the hands of Ahmad Shah, and though their great leader Mahdaji Sindia ruled at Delhi from 1784 onwards, the effort came too late, as the British by that time had ousted their most dangerous rivals, the French, and had consolidated their power in Bengal. The guardianship of India had passed from the Mahrattas to the British, and it was perhaps as well for the latter that Ahmad Shah had made no attempt to set up his own dynasty in India in place of that of Baber, but had been recalled to his Afghan dominions by domestic troubles and had left India in that state of anarchy in which he had found it. The Durani Empire, as founded by him, included Western Afghanistan and Baluchistan, to which the greater part of what is now the Punjab and Kashmir was tributary. After a reign of 26 years he was succeeded by his weak and dissolute son, Timur, under whom, as was only natural, the Empire fell to pieces. On Timur's death there was a scramble for the succession amongst his sons and other relatives, governors of the outlying provinces. Zaman Shah, Governor of Peshawar, the eldest and ablest of his sons, eventually obtained the throne. Following the example of his predecessors, he at once turned his attention towards India, and in 1796 advanced as far as Lahore, from which he threatened Delhi. The disorder induced by his appearance in India was so great that the British, as guardians of the peace of Bengal and Oudh, felt bound to take some defensive measures and in consequence troops were embodied to meet the expected attack. Fortunately Zaman Shah's attention was diverted by troubles in his own dominions, in which one of his brothers had rebelled against him, and he soon returned to Afghanistan. But the feeble resistance he encountered from the Sikhs aroused considerable misgivings in the minds of those in authority at Calcutta, and provoked a lengthy minute from Sir John Shore, at that time Governor-General. Cautious in this as in all his policy, that "most respectable servant of the Company[1]" came to no definite conclusion as to the measures to be taken by the British in order to guard against a recur-

[1] Malcolm's *History of India*, Vol. I. p. 119.

rence of the Afghan danger, and was quite undecided as to whether it were better for British
interests to support the Mahrattas against the
Afghans or to leave them to their fate. In the
latter case there might possibly arise a danger
from the French officers in the Mahratta service,
who, in the event of an Afghan defeat through
their instrumentality, might receive such an access
of power as would render them more dangerous
than either Mahrattas or Afghans. The British
Government could, in his opinion, do nothing but
await the course of events and was not called upon
to embark upon any expensive plan of defence[1].
This minute of Sir John Shore though thus incon-
clusive is of importance in two connexions. In the
first place it was only the beginning of a very long
series of despatches occasioned by dangers not from
powers within India but from those without. Great
Britain had by this time definitely taken up her
position as one of the great Indian powers, and the
defence of the whole peninsula from external invasion became a matter for her concern. Secondly, it
shadows forth that change of policy towards Oudh
which was to be consummated by Lord Wellesley.
In the recent outbreak the weakness of the Oudh
Government had been very clearly shewn, and
the advantages of attempting to strengthen the

[1] Malcolm's *History of India*, Vol. I. pp. 179 et seq.

Vizier's rule were becoming less and less obvious. Sir John Shore, though he fully recognised the military importance of Oudh, and on that account entered into closer relations with that state in his treaty of 1798, did nothing to remove the dangers consequent upon its wretched government, and it remained for Wellesley to reverse the policy upon which Warren Hastings had embarked, and by the annexation of Rohilcund to destroy the position of Oudh as a frontier state.

Zaman Shah's domestic troubles, in fomenting which Sir John Shore's successor, Lord Wellesley, had a hand, continued throughout his reign, and together with a threatened attack from Persia prevented his pursuing his schemes of Indian invasion. He had for the first time brought Afghanistan under the notice of the British Government, but Persia was to have the first claim on its attention for the next thirty years, and France, not Russia, to be the antagonist against whose aggression it desired to raise strong barriers. It endeavoured to do so by cultivating friendly relations with the Shah, to whom various missions were sent. The outcome of these was the Treaty of 1814, by which the Persian monarch bound himself to resist, by force or otherwise, the march of any European troops towards India, and to have no officers of any nation hostile to Great Britain in his service. The object of this treaty was to make the English dominions in the East safe from any attacks such as those proposed by the Russo-French alliances of 1800 and 1807, and its importance with regard to Afghan affairs lies in the fact that Great Britain was to help the Shah with arms and money in the case of any aggression from the west, and to defray the expenses of any army sent into Afghanistan at her desire. But the treaty had no practical results, for when with Napoleon's downfall all fears of French advances in the East vanished, Great Britain took the first opportunity of extricating herself from what now came to be regarded as a very bad bargain. This occurred in 1828, when Persia lay at Russia's mercy, and the Shah was in desperate need of money wherewith to pay a war indemnity. Great Britain was then released from all obligations under the treaty of 1814 upon payment of £300,000. In consequence British influence in Persia very rapidly declined, and the effects of the events of 1828 were soon seen in the Persian invasion of Herat in 1837, which furnished Lord Auckland with his great pretext for the first Afghan war, and which was undertaken at Russian instigation.

Meanwhile in Afghanistan were taking place events only too common in Oriental history.

Zaman Shah, unlike so many of the Moghul Emperors, had not followed the wise but bloodthirsty expedient of Shakespeare's Amurath, and had not upon his accession removed his brothers from his path. One of them, Mahomed Khan, deposed him and took possession of his kingdom, only in turn to be ousted by another and better known brother, Shah Shuja. With the latter the English opened relations in 1802. Mount-Stuart Elphinstone was sent on a mission to Kabul, of the splendours of which recollections were still lingering in Afghanistan thirty years later. The Shah, like every Afghan monarch before or since, was in need of money and demanded a subsidy, which was refused, but a treaty was nevertheless concluded. The French danger was, as we have seen, at this time uppermost in British minds, and the Shah promised to oppose, at the East India Company's cost, any attempt of the French to invade India by way of Afghanistan. But the treaty was hardly signed before another revolution drove Shah Shuja into exile and caused Great Britain to turn to Persia, instead of Afghanistan, for assistance against the French.

The exiled Afghan monarch applied to Ranjit-Singh for aid, but the crafty ruler of Lahore, putting into practice the principle that from him that hath not shall be taken even that which he hath, robbed him of the Kohinoor and sent him on to the East India Company, whose pensioner at Ludhiana he remained for the next twenty-three years. Mahomed Khan, his successor, soon became envious of the prominence of his energetic vizier, Fatteh Khan, who had twice raised him to the throne. At length with more than usual Oriental ingratitude he deposed, imprisoned, and tortured him But by so doing he raised up for himself a most formidable antagonist in the person of Fatteh Khan's younger brother, Dost Mahomed, who made himself Amir in 1826. His rule extended over Kabul and its neighbourhood, whilst his brothers held Kandahar as his vassals, and Kamran, Mahomed's son, retained possession of Herat, nominally as a fief from the Shah of Persia, with whom, however, his raids on Persian territory soon brought him into great disfavour. Shah Shuja made a fruitless attempt to recover his dominion in 1834 with the help of Ranjit Singh, who, always ready to make capital out of the misfortunes of others, took advantage of the disturbances in Afghanistan to seize Peshawar.

This summary of Afghan history is essential to the understanding of the policy which brought about the First Afghan War. The history of that war and of the diplomacy which led to it is perhaps the most unpleasant reading to be found in English annals, but some consideration of it is necessary because of the important influence it exercised on Afghan and Indian relations for the half-century which followed. Even now its remembrance has not altogether faded away.

Dost Mahomed was still smarting under the loss of Peshawar when Lord Auckland arrived in India in 1836. In the letter which he sent congratulating the new Governor-General on his accession, he asked him to communicate whatever might suggest itself to his mind for the settlement of the affairs of the country. The Dost was extremely desirous of Lord Auckland's assistance in coming to some arrangement with Ranjit Singh, by which Peshawar might be restored to Afghanistan. But Lord Auckland replied that it was not the practice of the British Government to interfere with the affairs of other independent states. In this he made his initial blunder. The Russian advance in Central Asia was already troubling him, though Russia was still more than a thousand miles from the borders of Afghanistan. The position which he took up in 1839, namely that a strong and friendly power on the North-West frontier was essential to the safety of the British dominion in India, was one in which he has been followed by every British statesman of note since. But before 1839 he had thrown away his opportunity of putting his doctrines into practice. This had been given him by the letter from Dost Mahomed to which he had replied so coldly. He had to his hand in that ruler an instrument for carrying out a wise and far-sighted policy such as rarely falls to a statesman's lot. For Dost Mahomed was a most remarkable man, greatly resembling his grandson Abdur Rahman in strength of character and faculty for dealing with men. During the thirty-seven years of his reign his throne was never really in danger for an instant, except at the hands of the British. Shah Shuja's unaided attack had troubled him but little, and might have convinced even the most sceptical that the Durani exile retained no hold on the affections of his former subjects. Moreover the Dost possessed, in addition to a strain of chivalry rare in the Afghan character (if we are to believe all that has been written of it), an admiration for the English, which, considering their treatment of him, is surprising. Had therefore Lord Auckland exercised a little tact in dealing with the differences between the Afghan ruler and Ranjit Singh he would have firmly attached Dost Mahomed to British interests. An arrangement with Ranjit Singh with regard to Peshawar would not have been difficult of accomplishment. For the Sikh ruler was quite willing to restore it to Dost Mahomed if the latter would hold it as a fief, and the Afghan, seeing the little love Ranjit Singh bore him, would have allowed it to be held by a brother upon whose fidelity he could not rely. A small subsidy to Ranjit Singh would have completed the business, and the money would have been much better spent in that manner than in pensioning exiles like Shah Shuja, who had no claims whatever upon the bounty of the East India Company. But Auckland would have none of it, and reproved Burnes—whose mission nominally commercial, but in reality political, compared but ill in the splendour which impresses the Oriental mind with that of Elphinstone in 1809—for exceeding his instructions by his offer of a subsidy to the Kandahar chiefs if they would abstain from an alliance with Persia. Disappointed in his hope of help from the British Government, Dost Mahomed sought it from Persia and Russia, as he had a perfect right to do, for even Auckland had acknowledged that Afghanistan was an independent state. The course of events is strangely similar to that which culminated in the second Afghan war. In each case the refusal of the Amir's requests brought about the entry of a Russian mission to Kabul, at which the British Government took umbrage and declared war. But Dost Mahomed was of a much less suspicious and exacting temperament than his son Shere Ali, and up till the end was willing to take a very little from England rather than a great deal from any other

power. A word of hope and encouragement from
Auckland would have sent Viktevich, the Russian
envoy, to the right about, and the little " encouragement and power" the Afghan ruler so humbly
asked for would have saved a fatuous war. Auckland, however, persisted in his impolitic course and
was confirmed in it by the Persian attack upon
Herat, then, as we have seen, no part of Afghanistan
proper, but even at that date regarded as the key
to India. Instigated no doubt as that attack was
by Russia, it is a wonder that it was so long delayed.
Kamran, the ruler of Herat, had brought it upon
himself by his cruel and audacious raids upon the
dominions of the Shah, his suzerain. But the gallant though somewhat overrated defence of the city
by Pottinger soon damped Persian military ardour,
and the Shah, only too anxious for an excuse to
retire, retreated hastily when a British force landed
on the island of Karrack in the Gulf of Persia.
Auckland was thus deprived of his only valid pretext for an Afghan invasion, as all danger to be
apprehended from Russia had ceased some little
time previously. That power, judging that the
time was not yet ripe for action, had disavowed its
agents, and Viktevich, rendered desperate by his
cold reception, had blown out his brains at Petersburg. The Governor-General would not withdraw,
perhaps because he was no longer in a position to

do so. His policy, he knew, had the approval of
the Home Government. In 1836 the action of
Persia began to arouse apprehension in the mind
of Palmerston, then Foreign Secretary, and in
reality head of the Melbourne ministry. An improbable story, resting on little more than bazaar gossip,
to the effect that negotiations were pending between
the courts of Kabul and Teheran with reference to
a partition of Kamran's territories and that the
Khan of Khiva was entering into engagements
with the Czar, caused him great uneasiness. It
was doubtless due to this that the Secret Committee
of the Court of Directors of the East India Company, the channel of communication between the
Home Government and the Governor-General, en-
joined upon Lord Auckland, at the outset of his
Governor-Generalship, a careful observation of
affairs in Afghanistan and Persia, and ordered him
to counteract the progress of Russian influence in
those countries either by a political or commercial
mission, as in his discretion might seem best,—a
curious anticipation of the instructions furnished
by Lord Salisbury to Lord Northbrook some forty
years later. These instructions are quite sufficient
to account for the frigid tone of Auckland's reply
to Dost Mahomed's application for advice and
assistance.

The next important communication of the

Home Government with reference to Afghan affairs
bears date May 10th, 1838.   In this Auckland was
informed that in consequence of the receipt of a
letter by Dost Mahomed from the Emperor Nicho-
las, Burnes must be ordered to withdraw from
Kabul, unless the Dost promised to refrain from
any further communication with Petersburg.   But
before this reached him, Auckland had reported on
May 22nd the withdrawal of Burnes from Kabul,
and had enclosed in this despatch the instructions
which he had given to MacNaghten with regard
to the negotiations with Ranjit Singh and Shah
Shuja which were to result in the Tripartite Treaty.
He also stated that the "emergency and the rapid
march of events" might compel him to act without
waiting for further instructions from London.   On
August 13th he informed the Secret Committee of
the result of MacNaghten's negotiations and assumed the entire responsibility for the restoration
of Shah Shuja.   Before this reached them, on Oct.
24th, 1838, two days before the arrival of Auckland's
previous despatch of May 22nd, the Secret Committee had declared that, as all efforts to cultivate
a closer acquaintance with Dost Mahomed had
failed, and as his brothers at Kandahar had thrown
themselves into the arms of a power whose approach to the Indus was incompatible with the
safety of her Majesty's Indian possessions, it

became an imperative duty to adopt a policy by which Kabul and Kandahar might be united under a sovereign bound to be a faithful ally of Great Britain. Shah Shuja fulfilled the required conditions, and though an insignificant effort, in their opinion, would be sufficient to restore him, Lord Auckland must take means to prevent all possibility of failure. Again, on November 9th, they observed, "You will have seen that, previous to the receipt of your advices, we had determined on recommending the course which you had, without any knowledge of our wishes, determined to pursue."

Thus whilst the responsibility for the restoration of Shah Shuja, which Auckland assumed on August 13th, would seem to rest by a very small margin of time with him alone, this correspondence with the Home authorities was not such as to create in him any desire to withdraw from his ill-fated enterprise. The only word of caution which reached him from London came in a letter of December 4th, in which the Committee expressed a hope that he would make every effort to conciliate Dost Mahomed, and that he was fully persuaded of Shah Shuja's ability to maintain himself without assistance from the British Government. This arrived too late to have any effect[1]. The

[1] For Lord Auckland's correspondence with the Home Government, see Keene's *History of India*, Vol. II. Appendix I.

Tripartite Treaty signed in 1838 between Shah
Shuja, Ranjit Singh, and the British (of which the
first-named got all the benefit, the last all the
burdens, whilst the Lion of Lahore gave the expedition little more than his benevolent approval)
arranged that Shah Shuja should be restored to
the throne of his ancestors, but British assistance
did not at present extend to the loan of British
troops. That, the crowning act of folly, was to
come later. Shah Shuja's own character made the
attempt to seat him on the throne of Afghanistan
a mad one. Weak and a coward, he contrasted
most unfavourably from every point of view with
the man who had indubitably proved his right to
rule Afghanistan by governing that country for
eleven years as it had never been governed before.
The promise of British troops made matters still
worse, and there were yet other circumstances
which added to the folly of the enterprise. Sind
and the Punjab formed no part of the British
dominions and were held by rulers proud of their
independence and most adverse to the passage of
British troops through their territories. The value
of Ranjit Singh's friendship was shewn by his
unwillingness to allow the British army to march
through the Punjab, the shortest route to its destination, and the greater of two evils therefore became a necessity, the troops, in defiance of all treaty

obligations, being sent by the much longer road through the country of the inoffensive Amirs of Sind. The difficulties of guarding the lines of communication in such a case are obvious, and were enhanced by the fact that Ranjit Singh died soon after the commencement of the expedition and the Punjab lapsed into a state of anarchy. Shah Shuja's popularity existed nowhere but in the minds of Auckland and his immediate advisers. It is most improbable that he would have reinstated himself at Kabul without the aid of British troops, but if he had attempted to do so there was a party in Afghanistan which would have rallied to his side. This he hopelessly alienated by accepting the help of British forces, and, by so doing, destroyed every chance of retaining the throne the British had won for him unless they remained to support him upon it. The Afghan, very sensitive on the score of national honour and extremely jealous of the interference of foreigners, was transformed into a bitter enemy of the returning exile and his allies.

It is unnecessary to dwell in detail upon the events of the next two years. All went well at first, and Auckland looked forward hopefully to the speedy withdrawal of the British troops which were in reality Shah Shuja's only prop and stay. Dost Mahomed's surrender in 1840 confirmed him in his

fatal optimism.   But this, to quote a phrase much
used in connexion with Afghan politics, was only
the calm before the storm.   The incapacity of the
head of the Indian Government was reflected in
every department, military and political, of the expedition he had sent forth.   In this case the policy
and the agents chosen to execute it were equally at
fault.   Men whose order of ability would have
enabled them to serve with credit in subordinate
positions and in time of peace, but absolutely
lacking the great powers, the initiative, and self-
reliance, necessary in critical situations, had been
selected to take charge of Afghan affairs.   Many
merits they undoubtedly possessed which could
have been utilised to the greatest advantage in
less troublous times, but in this particular instance
the merits of none compensated for the deficiencies
of others, and the result was an aggregate of the
most dangerous faults.   Unfortunately their incapacity met with its swift and terrible reward, and
an inglorious death saved them from surviving their
reputations.   Their failure and their regrettable
end shattered Auckland's castles in the air.   For
the first time, though not for the last, the Afghan
question became infinitely more important than
the Russian, of which it had formed originally but
a small part.   The only desire of the Governor-
General who succeeded Auckland was to get it off

his hands as quickly as was consistent with British honour. He was aided in his purpose by the fact that the melancholy incapacity displayed at Kabul had not been general, and two important Afghan strongholds were still in the British possession. Sale's defence of Jellalabad—though a more enterprising general would never have allowed himself to be cooped up in that town at all[1]—and Nott's of Kandahar were of the greatest service to Lord Ellenborough in his attempt to restore the damaged British prestige. The death of Shah Shuja, who was, of course, murdered immediately after his British supporters had left him, simplified matters, and, after the recovery of the captives and the occupation of Ghazni and Kabul, the British army was withdrawn. Lord Ellenborough had declared at the outset his intention of avenging British honour by the infliction of some signal defeat upon the Afghans, but, owing to his haste to evacuate the country, nothing was done to give its inhabitants any lasting impression of the might of Great Britain. The blowing up of the great Kabul bazaar, the noblest building of its kind in Central Asia, partook somewhat of the nature of an act of petty vengeance and was far more calculated to arouse hatred than fear.

Thus ended the first Afghan war. Dost Maho-

[1] Forbes, *Afghan Wars*, p. 69.

med was allowed to return to the kingdom from
which he ought never to have been ejected, but
there was no intercourse between him and the
British Government for thirteen years. During that
time he was left severely alone, notwithstanding
the fact that he gave the Sikhs assistance against
British troops in 1849. It is customary to take up
the thread of Afghan politics with the treaty of
1855, and, in dealing both with the war of 1878—
1881 and with the Afghan question of the present
day, but little reference is made to the events which
preceded 1855. This is a mistake. The position
in 1842 bore a superficial resemblance to that
of 1835. Dost Mahomed was, in both years,
in peaceful possession of Afghanistan, and his sentiments were, on the whole, quite friendly to the
British. But there was a fundamental difference.
However little the feelings of their ruler had altered,
and it is surprising that after his treatment at their
hands Dost Mahomed should have borne so little
animosity to the British, those of the people had
changed and they had learnt a lesson they were
not to be slow in repeating in the future. Mac-
Naghten, whose incurable optimism and absolute
refusal to believe that anything in which he had
a hand could possibly go wrong had caused his
whole moral nature to deteriorate most strangely
whilst in Afghanistan, had at any rate shewn them
that treachery and intrigue were not characteristics

of Afghans alone.   The British army, hitherto
invincible in Asia, had been subjected to a series
of humiliating disasters, and the Afghans could
clearly see the inestimable advantage the nature of
their country gave them.   The net result of the
campaign, so far as they were concerned, was to give
them a loathing for the British, who had endeavoured to force an unpopular monarch upon them,
and a contempt not altogether justified by the
circumstances for the military strength of their
enemies.   To us the first Afghan war is but a dark
spot in the annals of our history, which, whilst
we cannot view it without regret, loses its black-
ness in the light of other achievements.   But to the
Afghans it meant something very different.   In
the first trial of strength between them and the
great Empire to the south-west they had almost, if
not quite, held their own, and the result was to fill
them with that overweening sense of the importance of themselves and their ruler which was to
stand Shere Ali in such evil stead.

This was the effect of the war upon the Afghans.
In relation to subsequent British diplomacy it is
no less important.   The Russian question remained
for a time in the background.   It slumbered and
slept until fresh and unmistakable Russian advances
in Central Asia aroused British statesmen into
action once more.   Exactly what to do they did
not know.   For years they had been chary of

dealings with Afghanistan for fear of again getting
their fingers burnt.   A spirit of despair had come
over them.   They did not quite accurately estimate
the lack of statesmanship and military capacity
displayed by Auckland and his subordinates.   For
his successors the situation was decidedly not that
of 1836.   A tide had passed which had not been
taken at the flood, and the failure of a policy
which, however evil in itself, in the hands of other
agents might have turned out very differently, was
made an excuse for no settled policy at all and for
dealing with events as they occurred.   Masterly
inactivity, or—in less polite phraseology—doing
nothing, may seem a settled policy, but the policy
pursued during the next two generations was not
even inactivity.   The war of 1839—1842 is responsible for most of the vacillations and disputes
of the next forty years.   That some control over
Afghan affairs and some understanding on the
subject with Russia were necessary was recognized
by all the most experienced Anglo-Indian statesmen.   But the measures taken to bring about either
of these desirable consummations were most half-
hearted, and the result was a policy of drift, of which
war was the inevitable outcome.   The events of
1842—1875 were as much responsible for the
second Afghan war as any part of Lord Lytton's
policy.   These events were in a great measure the
legacy Lord Auckland left India.

CHAPTER III.

FROM THE END OF THE FIRST AFGHAN WAR TO THE BEGINNING OF LORD LYTTON'S GOVERNOR-GENERALSHIP (1842—1875).

Affairs at Herat.—The Treaties of 1855 and 1857 with Dost Mahomed.—Discussion of the question of a British envoy at the Court of Kabul.—Effect of the Treaty of 1857.—Dost Mahomed's action during the Mutiny.—His Death.—Anarchy in Afghanistan.—Succession of Shere Ali.—Criticism of Sir John Lawrence's Policy.—The Forward Policy.—Sir Henry Rawlinson's minute.—Sir John Lawrence's reply.—The Umballa Conference.—Its results.—Boundary Negotiations between Great Britain and Russia.—The Afghan-Russian Correspondence.—The Sistan Boundary Commission.—Shere Ali's dissatisfaction at its award.—The Simla Conference.—Rebellion of Yakub Khan.—Change of Government in England.—Disraeli's Orientalism.—Change of policy towards Afghanistan.—Resignation of Lord Northbrook.

It is not easy to judge the statesmanship of the past, for whilst the novice can often see after any great disaster the way in which it might have been averted, to the statesman who brought it about such a result seemed most unlikely to follow upon his policy. For, after all, it is impossible to see much further ahead in politics than in meteorology, and the greatest statesman is perhaps he who takes the most firm and consistent line in dealing with the contingencies of the moment, whilst studying each carefully in its relation to the past and future. Such a course was not however adopted by those who had the management of Afghan affairs in the middle of the last century.

As we have seen, for thirteen years there was no communication between Afghanistan and the British Government. Dost Mahomed spent the time in consolidating his dominions, taking possession of Balkh and Kandahar, which had previously been held by his brothers. Yar Mahomed, prime minister to Kamran, ruler of Herat, had, as is so frequently the case in Oriental states, ousted his master and reigned in his stead. In 1851 his successor offered to become a vassal of Persia, but in 1853 the latter kingdom was compelled by Great Britain to sign a treaty recognizing the independence of Herat. Dost Mahomed, however, to the safety of whose dominions the possession of Herat meant much, in alarm at the encroachments of Persia drew nearer to Great Britain and demanded a treaty. John Lawrence, then Chief Commissioner of the Punjab, was very doubtful of the wisdom of acceding to his request, as he

thought any entanglement in Afghan affairs, however slight, most undesirable. But in 1855 a treaty
was signed by him and by Gholam Hyder Khan,
Dost Mahomed's son and heir-apparent. The
treaty is a very short one and extremely one-
sided. It furnishes another illustration of Dost
Mahomed's willingness to take a little from Great
Britain in preference to a great deal from elsewhere. It engaged that, between the East India
Company and Dost Mahomed and his heirs, there
should be perpetual peace and friendship, and that
the East India Company should respect the territories then in the Amir's possession and should
never interfere therein, the Amir to do the like for
the territories of the East India Company and to
be the friend of its friends and the enemy of its
enemies[1]. The second of these provisions acquired
a somewhat fictitious importance at a later time
from the fact that Herat at this date formed no
part of the Dost's dominions, and that the promise
of non-interference in them could not therefore
be held to apply to it. Such an interpretation is
decidedly against the spirit, if not the letter, of the
treaty, and it is extremely doubtful whether it was
really held by Lord Lytton or any of his supporters. The third clause is the one which gives
the treaty the one-sided character of which Shere

[1] *Afghan Blue Book* (1), 1878, p. 1.

Ali so bitterly complained. Engagements between a barbarous and a civilized state have always many disadvantages, and it certainly is not for the benefit of the latter to promise the former its support under all circumstances. But if such engagements are entered into, there should be some attempt at reciprocity, and too much should not be expected from the weaker power. Dost Mahomed, however, seemed quite content, but was soon in fresh difficulties. Persia in spite of all warnings had seized Herat, whilst there was considerable disaffection in many parts of his dominions, especially in Kandahar and Balkh. He therefore again appealed for British aid and wished to come to Peshawar in person. Lawrence, in pursuance of his policy of non-interference, was unwilling that he should do so, but the Governor-General, Lord Dalhousie, consented, not being desirous of risking the Amir's disaffection. The result was a second treaty which, with the exception of the seventh article, was avowedly temporary in character. The fourth and seventh articles are the only ones which have any importance in connexion with our present purpose. By the fourth, the Amir engaged to receive British officers at Kabul, Balkh, and Kandahar, whose functions were to be solely military. They were to see that the subsidy to be paid to the Amir was properly spent, and to keep their

Government informed of "all affairs." But they were not to interfere in any way in the internal administration of the country and, by the seventh article, were to be withdrawn at the conclusion of the war: at the pleasure of the British Government, a Vakil, not a European officer, might however remain at Kabul, and one at Peshawar on the Amir's part[1]. Lawrence, knowing the Amir's dislike to the presence of British officers in his dominions, promised not to press this point, unless absolutely necessary, and no officers were ever sent to Kabul. He had evidently been persuaded by the Amir himself of the difficulties which stood in the way, for Dost Mahomed said afterwards to Lumsden, the head of the mission to Kandahar which had so much to do with keeping the Amir faithful during the troublous times of the Mutiny:—

"Jan Larrens wanted you to go to Kabul and impressed on me the necessity of your doing so, but I pointed out to him the impossibility of it, for you see, Lumsden Sahib, that although I might delight to have you there, yet I have under surveillance in Kabul all the bad characters in the country with their followers, and you know how —— and others would rejoice to bring me into trouble by putting a bullet in you or any of the

[1] *Afghan Blue Book* (1), 1878, p. 2.

other Sahibs. There is no reason why you should not be with me in Kabul or in any other place in Afghanistan except my want of power to protect you there, and it must not be[1]."

Here perhaps will be the best place to discuss the whole question of a British representative at the court of Kabul which has so important a bearing upon subsequent Afghan history. Doubtless it would be greatly to the advantage of the British Government, in its dealings with Afghanistan, to have a British agent at the Amir's court, to whom would be possible a clearer conception of the policy of the British Government than could be possessed by any native of India, and who would be free from racial and, above all, from religious prejudices. A Mahomedan, however great his fidelity to British interests, can scarcely be expected to forego his allegiance to the cause of Islam or to be alive to all the faults of a ruler of his own faith. But the difficulties from the Afghan point of view are almost insurmountable, though they have decreased with the lapse of time. In the first place there is the character of the nation. Proud, fanatical, and very suspicious of foreigners, the Afghans have not, even yet, quite outlived the days when to slay an infidel

[1] *Lumsden of the Guides*, p. 139; *Quarterly Review*, 1900, p. 479.

was a deed worthy of Paradise, and the property of the slain a small, though justly earned, reward for the killing. Afghanistan, at the present time, notwithstanding the great strides it has made in recent years, is but a half-civilized country, and in the middle of the last century it was little in advance of Bokhara or Tibet. In addition to the difficulties on the part of the people which stood, and still stand, in the way of the appointment of a British envoy to Kabul, there are others and still more potent ones on the part of the ruler. It is improbable that, even had the Amir sent an Afghan envoy to Peshawar in accordance with the treaty of 1857, he would have been any the more willing to receive a British officer at Kabul. In the first place, as we have seen, he could not guarantee his safety. That however is not the greatest drawback from the Amir's point of view. The acceptance of such an envoy would seem to him to imply degradation to the level of the native Indian princes. The argument that, if he received a British envoy, Russia would also demand the reception of one has little weight now so far as the Amir is concerned. The question as to whether a Russian should follow a British embassy at Kabul has passed from his decision to that of the two great neighbouring Governments. It had, however, very considerable force in Shere Ali's time.

It was of smaller consequence to the Dost, as, throughout his reign, Russia was at a considerable distance from his borders. But to Shere Ali, who had been exhorted by Lords Mayo and Northbrook to treat the communications of the Russian Government in a friendly spirit, and who had no reason to believe that the British Government viewed Russia's advance with anything but approval, it must have seemed a much more important matter. Such a demand would only double his difficulties. Finally, he knew quite as well as the greater rulers who preceded and followed him that there are many Oriental methods which do not recommend themselves to European minds, and that a British envoy might report with strong disfavour punishments which he himself rather admired as most exactly fitting the crime. Many of the proceedings of Eastern courts will not bear the light of day. Of this Shere Ali received a sharp reminder when, although there was no British mission at his court, Lord Northbrook ventured to rebuke him for his treacherous dealings with his son Yakub, and the protest, courteous and dignified though it was, could not but fail to make him sensible that worse things might happen if a British mission once set foot in his capital. On these grounds he pertinaciously resisted all demands that the relations between himself and the British Government should be placed on a different footing.

The object of the treaty of 1857 was soon accomplished. Herat was saved from Persia and handed over to Ahmad Khan, the Amir's nephew. Afghan affairs were obscured for the next few years in the great upheaval of the Mutiny. It was as well for the British Government that its relations with Dost Mahomed had become closer in the years which preceded 1858, for he was sorely tempted by many of his subjects, and especially his favourite son, Shere Ali, to add to its difficulties and as head of the Mahomedan faith to proclaim a jehad against the infidel. Such an opportunity to recover Peshawar, which he coveted so eagerly, might not occur again. Indeed he bade fair at one time to obtain it in a more peaceful manner ; for, had any disaster happened at Delhi during the Mutiny, the British would probably have handed it over to him and retreated beyond the Indus. But, thanks to John Lawrence, whose idea this was, there was no disaster at Delhi, which together with the rest of the Punjab he held throughout that stormy time in the hollow of his hand. And the Dost, partly owing to the persuasion of his second son Azim—to whom in after years the British debt was but scantily repaid— who saw the inevitable end of the struggle, and partly owing to his own native loyalty of character, held firmly to his engagements, and, in consequence, our recovery in India was much more speedy than it otherwise might have been.

In 1862 the Amir, with the tacit permission of the British Government, marched against Herat and, whilst bringing the siege of that city to a successful conclusion, died under its walls. The fact was reported to Lord Elgin by Shere Ali, but the Governor-General's death prevented his taking the necessary steps to acknowledge Dost Mahomed's successor formally. Sir William Denison, who acted as Governor-General pending the arrival of Sir John Lawrence, did this, but the recognition was not a very prompt one[1]. Lord Elgin had delayed it at the outset until further news was received from Afghanistan, and his death again postponed it. Whether a more speedy recognition would have had any effect in preventing the internecine struggles which now ensued it is difficult to say. Shere Ali was opposed by his two elder brothers Afzal and Azim. For two years he held the Amirship in a precarious way, but after his defeat in May, 1866, by Abdur Rahman at Sharkabad, Afzal was proclaimed Amir. His brother Azim was, however, the real ruler, for Afzal was, as Sir John Lawrence said, a sot and

[1] *Afghan Blue Book* (1), 1878, pp. 3 and 8.

an imbecile. At the beginning of 1867 Shere Ali
was compelled to evacuate Kandahar. Lawrence,
now Governor-General, had acknowledged Afzal as
Wali of Kabul and afterwards as Amir of Kabul
and Kandahar, but had declared that he would
continue to recognize Shere Ali as ruler of those
territories of which he was in actual possession.
The position is complicated for the moment
by the fact that Shere Ali, despairing of help
from the British, shewed an inclination to make
overtures to Persia[1]. As this was a breach of
the treaty of 1855, to which he had declared his
adherence, Lawrence suggested that it would be
in the interests of British India to assist openly
the party in power at Kabul with money and
arms against him. But Shere Ali's star was only
temporarily eclipsed. He was by far the ablest
of the three brothers, and his rivals played
into his hands by their arbitrary proceedings at
Kabul. Azim, who had been virtual ruler there
throughout his brother's reign and who had succeeded to the throne at his death, was detested
because of his cruel exactions and savage execu-
tions, whilst Abdur Rahman, whose inclinations
were for a milder policy, had no influence. Shere
Ali therefore, consolidating his power at Herat,
soon found himself equal to another contest, and

[1] *Afghan Blue Book* (1), 1878, p. 20.

by January, 1869, had made himself undisputed
ruler over a larger territory than had been held
by his father.

The anarchy, which at this time prevailed in
Afghanistan, is important because the policy pursued by the British Government towards it formed
the subject of much discussion. The proper course
to be followed in dealing with the contending
factions which inevitably spring up on the death
of the ruler of such a state as Afghanistan, to the
throne of which there is no definite law of succession, will be more fitly discussed in dealing
with the future relations between that country
and the British Empire in India. The whole
question is an extremely difficult one, but one
factor which now enters into it, the contiguity of
the Russian and Afghan dominions, was absent
in 1863. Hence it was at this time, perhaps, the
safer and wiser plan to let the contesting parties
fight out their own quarrels. This at any rate was
what Lawrence did, in accordance with a desire
Dost Mahomed had expressed to him in 1857[1].
The formal acknowledgment of Shere Ali had
taken place before Lawrence became Governor-
General and so he was in no way responsible
for it. His successive recognitions of the various
Amirs may not seem a particularly dignified

[1] *Afghan Blue Book* (1), 1878, p. 60.

course, and it is obvious that moral recognition without material support is of particularly little use and might indeed be a serious drawback to a pretender to the Afghan throne. Lawrence's action had, however, at least this in its support that it was in accordance with existing treaties. But there were two occasions on which Lawrence departed from his rigid rule of non-interference. Had the assistance he suggested in view of Shere Ali's overtures to Persia been given to Shere Ali himself earlier, it would probably have prevented his losing his kingdom, had it been given to Azim later it would probably have prevented his ever regaining it. Shere Ali's advances to Persia gave Lawrence the excuse for helping one of the contending Afghan parties in the one case which was perhaps lacking in the other. The assistance given to Shere Ali in 1869 was due to one of two reasons—but as to which it was, the supporters and antagonists of the so-called Forward policy usually settle as best pleases themselves. It may have been due to Sir Henry Rawlinson's minute of 1868, or, on the other hand, to the fact that Shere Ali was at last in possession, and was occupying a stronger position than had any claimant to the throne since 1863. The subsidy was in consequence paid him as a reward for putting an end to a state of anarchy in Afghanistan unfavourable to British interests—a result, as Lawrence pointed out, solely due to his own courage, ability, and firmness[1]. To this Shere Ali, in view of his unavailing attempts to get assistance from Great Britain, scarcely needed his attention drawn. But if we take into consideration Lawrence's policy as a whole, and especially his comments upon Sir Henry Rawlinson's proposals, the second of the two suggested above would seem the more probable solution.

Sir Henry Rawlinson's minute, sent to the Government of India by order of the Secretary of State in 1868, is of considerable, though perhaps somewhat exaggerated importance in the history of Afghan politics as it marks the beginning of what has been labelled the Forward policy. The line between two apparently antagonistic policies is often very finely drawn, and it is extremely difficult to say in what exactly the Forward policy consisted, especially as it went through many phases under different statesmen. The term too has been used in two slightly differing connexions, namely in reference to the Indian frontier as well as to Afghanistan itself. Its gist however may be described as a demand for the consolidation of the Indian Empire right up to the furthest Afghan borders, a consolidation which necessitated the

---

[1] *Afghan Blue Book* (1), 1878, p. 43.

attainment of a paramount position both on the Indian frontier and beyond it, in Afghanistan.

Compared with the later developments of the Forward policy under Lord Lytton, Sir Henry Rawlinson's proposals are extremely moderate. He recommended that some steps should be taken to counteract the Russian advance in Central Asia and prophesied that advance much on the lines on which it has actually taken place. His minute is not, as a matter of fact, unduly alarmist in tone. The active measures he advised, which concern us more particularly here, were that Shere Ali should be strengthened and subsidised at Kabul, our position at that capital being rendered secure and paramount, the re-establishment of our influence in Persia, and the occupation and fortification of Quetta[1]. That the diplomatic interference in Afghanistan which was, of necessity, the outcome of his first proposal should be by means of a British envoy at its court he nowhere suggests.

If we take Sir John Lawrence's consideration of these suggestions as typical of the opposing school, we get a clear statement of the antagonistic policies, of which that pursued at the present day, while still possessing many disadvantages, is in some ways a judicious blend. The subject of the Russian advance had not been altogether neglected

[1] *Afghan Blue Book* (1), 1878, pp. 31—41.

by Lawrence. In the communication to the Home Government to which reference has been already made, in which Shere Ali's dealings with Persia were discussed, he had advocated an "understanding and even an engagement with Russia" with regard to the border line of the spheres of influence of the two great Empires in Central Asia[1]. But his representations were unheeded, and in Sir Stafford Northcote's reply he was told that the Home Government saw no reason for any uneasiness or any jealousy[2]. He again returned to the subject in his minute upon Sir Henry Rawlinson's proposal. This is a careful exposition of his policy and acquits him altogether of the charge of masterly inactivity[3]. He was very mistrustful of any interference in Afghan affairs, in which he thought we should be embroiling ourselves indefinitely; for he regarded it as extremely improbable that there would ever be, for any extended period, a strong and united Government in Afghanistan. He thought the British Government's wisest course would be to consolidate its rule in India, and to entrench itself securely behind its natural boundaries. He was therefore opposed to the occupation of Quetta. He expressed his

[1] *Afghan Blue Book* (1), 1878, p. 20.

[2] *Ibid.*, p. 25.

[3] *Ibid.*, pp. 60 *et seq.*

firm opinion that a native agent alone was possible
at Kabul, and that Lumsden had been in considerable danger in 1857.   But above all, he laid down
the principle that Russia, not Afghanistan, was the
country with which we must concern ourselves, and,
whilst admitting that the danger anticipated in that
direction might never arise, thought that nothing
was to be gained in fortifying ourselves against it
by any interference in the affairs of Afghanistan.
The Home Government's best policy was to "endeavour to come to some mutual arrangement and
to an understanding with Russia, and failing that,
we might give that power to understand that an
advance towards India beyond a certain point
would entail on her war in all parts of the world
with England[1]."

We have then, in these two minutes, two definite
declarations of policy which it is important to consider in connexion with the events of the next ten
years.   Had either of these policies been followed
vigorously from the time they were offered to the
consideration of the Home Government, the complications of a later date would have been avoided.
But this was not the case, and the result was half-
and-half measures which failed to effect any useful object.   The actual policy of the next two
Governor-Generals, forced upon them often, it is

[1] *Afghan Blue Book* (1), 1878, pp. 60 *et seq.*

true, by the Home Government, may best be described as a whittling down of Lord Lawrence's. But what had been lost was infinitely the more important part of his policy, namely, the clear understanding with Russia. The Home Government in the most lifeless way approached Russia on the subject of Afghanistan, remained content with the latter's assurance that Afghanistan was regarded by the Czar as entirely outside his sphere of influence, and settled in an extremely perfunctory manner the boundary of the Amir's dominions. But it did nothing in the matter of making Russia understand that any infringement of that boundary on her part would mean war, nor did it endeavour to embody the plausible Russian assurances in any formal agreement.

Failing this, which, in the light of more recent events, would have been infinitely the wiser arrangement, the proper course would have been to discard Lawrence's policy altogether in favour of Rawlinson's and to have entered into much closer relations with the ruler of Afghanistan. This too was not done. Lawrence's rule of non-interference was accepted to the full, having lost altogether its *raison d'être*. In consequence the way was most successfully paved for Lord Lytton's greater blunders.

Lawrence left India soon after writing his minute, but not before he had given instructions

N.   4

that a supply of arms and ammunition together
with six lakhs of rupees should be forwarded to
Shere Ali.   He was not unwilling that, whilst
preventive measures should be taken with regard
to Russia, Shere Ali should be conciliated as far
as possible.   This was to be done by a small
subsidy to be continued during good behaviour,
more especially with regard to the frontier tribes.
An offensive and defensive alliance was not to be
thought of, as it would lead the Amir to make
excessive demands upon the British, and, if those
were denied, to repudiate all his engagements.   Still
it was desirable "that our relations with him should
confer lasting benefits, and that he should feel certain we were interested in the safety of his country[1]."

These were the principles Lawrence left for the
guidance of his successors.   He had hoped to meet
the Amir but was prevented from doing so, and
Shere Ali did not visit British territory until 1869.
In the March of that year took place the Umballa
Conference.   The magnificence of his reception
afforded Shere Ali much pleasure, but he received
little tangible benefit from a meeting for which he
had left his country at a critical time, for as yet his
throne was by no means secure.   In the letter he
received from Lord Mayo embodying the results

[1] Sir John Lawrence's Minute, *Afghan Blue Book* (1), 1878,
pp. 60 *et seq.*

of the conference[1], he was told that the British Government would regard with severe displeasure any attempts on the part of his rivals to disturb his position, and that it would endeavour by such means as circumstances might require to strengthen his government, to enable him to exercise with equity and justice his rightful rule, and to transmit to his descendants all the dignities and honours of which he was the lawful possessor. He was to communicate freely with the British Government on all matters of interest.

Very vague and shadowy indeed were these promises, and very unsatisfactory they must have appeared to one who had come demanding a *de jure* acknowledgment of himself and his successors, an offensive and defensive alliance, an annual subsidy, and a recognition of Abdullah Jan, his favourite son, as heir presumptive. The lack of definiteness was most apparent in the promise to view with severe displeasure any attacks upon Shere Ali's position. Of what service that would have been to him is by no means clear since it was carefully explained to him that the British Government had no intention of interfering actively to suppress any risings against him. But indeterminate as Lord Mayo's letter was, it was too clear-cut for the Duke of Argyle, then Secretary of State

[1] *Afghan Blue Book* (1), 1878, p. 90.

for India, who feared to go even thus far[1]. Shere
Ali had complained with considerable justice of
the one-sided character of the treaty of 1855, and
surely if it were desirable to have any close relations
at all with the ruler of Afghanistan, something
might have been done to place them on a more
equal footing. Argyle went still further in the
course of giving little and demanding much, and
thought Lord Mayo had promised more than he
should have done. However he declared himself
satisfied with the Governor-General's explanations.
Lord Mayo summed up the results of the conference as follows :—

"1st. What the Amir is not to have—

"No treaty, no fixed subsidy, no European
troops, officers or residents, no dynastic pledges.

"2nd. What he is to have—

"Warm countenance and support, discourage-
ment of his rivals, such material assistance as we
may consider absolutely necessary for his immediate wants, constant and friendly communication
through our Commissioner at Peshawar and our
native agents in Afghanistan[2]."

The first of these articles is badly expressed,
and in later years gave a handle to those who
wished to send a British resident to Kabul, in that

[1] *Afghan Blue Book* (1), 1878, p. 92.
[2] *Ibid.*, p. 95.

it mingles indiscriminately the objects on which the Amir had set his heart—the treaty, the fixed subsidy, the dynastic pledges—with an object for which he had not the least desire, the European troops, officers or residents.

Shere Ali returned to Afghanistan with what satisfaction he could find in the Governor-General's promises of warm countenance and support. But though his journey, undertaken at a most inconvenient time for himself, had been practically fruitless, the Umballa Conference was by no means a failure. It illustrated very completely what the personality of one man could effect. Lord Mayo's charm of manner and magnificent courtesy made a deep impression upon the mind of the impulsive Amir and made him the Governor-General's warm personal friend. He left India moderately contented, and for the next year or two endeavoured to carry out loyally the promises he had made of better rule.

During the year 1869 negotiations began between Russia and Great Britain with regard to the Central Asian question[1]. Prince Gortschakoff and Lord Clarendon were the principals, and the result of their deliberations was that Shere Ali was acknowledged by Russia as ruler of all the territories then in his possession. He was to abstain from

[1] *Afghan Blue Book* (1), 1878, pp. 104, 105.

all interference in Bokhara, and the Amir of the
latter country was not to meddle in Afghanistan.
Lord Clarendon had started with the idea of a
neutral zone, but after studying the question had
come to the somewhat obvious conclusion that
Afghanistan did not fulfil the necessary conditions
for such a zone, and had proposed that the Oxus
should be the boundary line between the spheres
of influence of the two Empires, Afghanistan remaining completely outside that of Russia. Prince
Gortschakoff consented, stating that he saw no objection to British officers visiting Kabul, though he
agreed with the Earl of Mayo that Russian agents
should not do so. It remained then to settle the
boundaries of Afghanistan. This was not done till
1873, Lord Clarendon having in the meantime
been succeeded by Lord Granville. Even then the
boundary was not determined in a very satisfactory
manner, there being apparently as much doubt
concerning the exact source of the Oxus as about
that of the Nile or Niger.

Both the Home and Indian Governments were
perfectly, though very easily, satisfied with the
Russian assurances that that country would adhere
to the policy of extending its territory no further in
Central Asia as it considered extension of territory
an extension of weakness. The Russian Government also declared that the occupation of Khiva

was not intended to be permanent[1]. Shere Ali
himself was the person who most thoroughly dis-
trusted the Russians, and a letter which he had
received from General Kauffman, Governor of Turkestan, explaining Abdur Rahman's presence at
Tashkent caused him great uneasiness. This was
to some extent removed by Lord Mayo, who somewhat unwisely told the Amir that "these letters will
be, when rightly understood, a source of confidence
to your Highness[2]." The first letters were, it is
true, harmless enough, but a correspondence between a Russian Governor and the ruler of a country
altogether outside Russia's sphere of influence was
not a thing to be encouraged. Russia would have
strongly resented any letters from Lord Mayo to
the Amir of Bokhara, over whom Prince Gortschakoff admitted that the Russian Government had
less influence than the British over the Afghan
ruler[3]. The British Government should have clearly
intimated to Prince Gortschakoff that the only
channel of communication between Russia and
Afghanistan of which it approved was the Governor-
General of India. Unfortunately this was not done,
and thus was laid the foundation for much of Shere
Ali's subsequent estrangement.

[1] *Afghan Blue Book* (1), 1878, pp. 101, 107.
[2] Hanna, *Second Afghan War*, p. 28.
[3] *Afghan Blue Book* (1), 1878, p. 104.

Between 1869 and 1872 other events happened
which were to bring about trouble in the near
future. Shortly before his tragic death Lord Mayo
had persuaded Shere Ali to submit to arbitration
the question of the province of Sistan, on which for
many years Persia had been making gradual encroachments. The result was unfortunate, and it
would probably have been better to let the parties
fight the matter out. The expenditure of blood
and treasure would have been small and both Persia
and Afghanistan would have been better satisfied.
Arbitration does not appeal to the Oriental mind,
nor did this particular award tend to increase Shere
Ali's belief in that method of settling disputes.
For it was a poor attempt at a compromise. The
disputed territory was decided between the two
claimants, but that portion—up to the Helmund—
granted to Afghanistan was by no means com-
parable in fertility with the country gained by
Persia. The award still further added to Shere
Ali's sense of injury as by it he lost a strong
strategic point. His first attempt at extracting
benefit from the warm countenance and support of
his British friends was thus attended with signal
failure.

Before the award of the Sistan boundary commission was made public, Lord Mayo had been
assassinated, and by his death the link of personal

friendship which bound Shere Ali to India was snapped. The new Governor-General was in the particular respect which had attracted Shere Ali to Lord Mayo a striking contrast to his predecessor. He was somewhat cold and reserved, and entirely lacking in the personal glamour by which Lord Mayo had been able to win Shere Ali. He was, however, prepared to be a good friend to Shere Ali as far as might be allowed both by that ruler himself and by the Home Government. His first step was a proposal to the Amir that a British envoy, Macnabb, should be sent to Kabul to explain the results both of the Sistan boundary award and of the late negotiations with Russia. This fact is worthy of notice as it is sometimes erroneously stated that the Simla Conference was the outcome of a wish expressed by Shere Ali on his own initiative. It was, however, suggested by him in order that he might avoid receiving a British envoy in Afghanistan. He did not actually decline to do so, but before receiving the envoy he was anxious to know the general terms of the Sistan award, and exactly what the Governor-General proposed to do regarding the safety and consolidation of his kingdom. His own proposal regarding the Simla meeting he put forward as an alternative to the Governor-General's; but in a private letter from the British Vakil at Kabul, Atta Mahomed Khan, it was made clear that the Afghan Durbar very much disliked the idea of a British envoy and that, had the Governor-General pressed the proposal, it would probably have been refused point-blank. However it was not pressed, and Syad Nur Mahomed was sent to meet the Governor-General at Simla. Other things than the Sistan boundary award were there discussed. First of all, the Afghan envoy enlarged upon Shere Ali's growing distrust of Russia and his desire to draw nearer to England[1]. Whether his fears of the Russian advance were intentionally exaggerated it is impossible to say, but at any rate they failed in their object. It may be true that Shere Ali misinterpreted the very vague promises of Lords Lawrence and Mayo and thought they meant much more than was actually the case; but it is also true that he had more reason to fear Russia in 1873 than in 1869, and that he was therefore entitled to press for something more definite. Lord Northbrook saw this and telegraphed to the Duke of Argyle asking permission to assure the Amir that, "if he unreservedly accepts and acts upon our advice in all external relations, we will help him, with money, arms, and troops if necessary, to repel an unprovoked invasion; we to be the judge of the necessity[2]." This was not

---

[1] *Afghan Blue Book* (1), 1878, p. 109.
[2] *Ibid.*, p. 108.

much and was very far from being the offensive and
defensive alliance which Shere Ali had demanded
in 1869, but, such as it was, it was going a great
deal too far for the cautious mind of the Secretary
of State, who telegraphed back that "the Cabinet
thinks that you should inform the Amir that we do
not at all share his alarm and consider there is no
cause for it : but you may assure him that we shall
maintain our settled policy in favour of Afghanistan
if he abides by our advice in external affairs[1]."
This telegram can in no sense be regarded as
sanctioning the Governor-General's extremely
moderate proposals, and the results of the Simla
Conference so far as Shere Ali was concerned were
summed up in his letter to Lord Northbrook of
Nov. 18th, 1873[2]. In this he expressed his deep
dissatisfaction at the Sistan award, which he regarded as inconsistent with the Treaty of Paris. He
added, that if Lord Northbrook only intended to
continue the policy of his two immediate predecessors, there had been no need for the Simla Conference. He concluded with a protestation of his
continued friendship. In spite of the latter there
can be no doubt that the result of the conference
was a great blow to him. He had got absolutely
nothing from it except ten lakhs of rupees—five of

[1] *Afghan Blue Book* (1), 1878, p. 108.
[2] *Ibid.*, p. 119.

which were compensation to his subjects for claims
relative to Sistan—and a supply of rifles. The
latter he accepted, the former he declined, thus
shewing the extent of his chagrin. The whole
progress of the late negotiations had served to
convince him that Afghan interests were a purely
secondary consideration with the British Government, and that he could only expect help if it
suited the plans and convenience of that Government. Shere Ali was, it must be admitted, a difficult man to deal with, and many of his troubles
were of his own seeking. Proud, jealous, implacable
and treacherous, he had far too great a sense of
his own importance. In addition, he possessed
anything but a well-balanced mind, as is shewn by
the fits of excessive grief, falling but little short of
temporary insanity, into which he was thrown by
the deaths of his two favourite sons. Nevertheless
the results of the Simla Conference might have
been much more satisfactory, both from his point
of view and from that of the British. Half confidence is often worse than none at all, and at Simla
the last opportunity of placing our relations with
the Amir on a firmer basis was thrown away.

The estrangement thus begun was soon to be
augmented. In the later months of 1873 Abdullah Jan was definitely acknowledged by Shere Ali
as heir presumptive. The Governor-General coldly

expressed his good wishes to the new heir, but said nothing more, as the step was one of which he did not approve[1]. Yakub Khan, the Amir's eldest son, was persuaded by his father's specious promises to visit Kabul, but immediately on arrival there was thrown into prison. This step Lord Northbrook reproved—from a political point of view somewhat injudiciously. He strongly advised the Amir to observe the conditions under which Yakub had come to Kabul. By so doing he would maintain his good name and the friendship of the British Government[2]. This reproof was much resented by Shere Ali and his Durbar. To the Amir it seemed a breach of the agreement that the British Government should not interfere in the internal affairs of Afghanistan, and he could see nothing blameworthy in his recent conduct. He had treated his brother Afzal in that manner, and why not now his son? Such a method of ridding himself of an unfilial son, who was a troublesome nuisance, merited praise rather than censure, and in disapproving it the Governor-General scarcely shewed his "warm friendship and countenance." Such an incident tended but little to increase his good feeling towards his exacting British neighbours, although in acknowledging the Governor-General's letter he declared that it was

---

[1] *Afghan Blue Book* (1), 1878, p. 118.
[2] *Ibid.*, p. 126.

being "confirmed and consolidated every hour and every minute[1]."

Meanwhile a change of Government had taken place in England which was to be fraught with serious consequences to Afghanistan. In March, 1874, Mr Gladstone was succeeded as Prime Minister by Mr Disraeli, and Lord Salisbury became Secretary of State for India. Over the mind of Disraeli as over that of Burke the East exercised a strange fascination. But there was a radical difference between the "Orientalism" of the two statesmen. That of Burke resolved itself into a well-intentioned but fierce and by no means always wise championship of a nation with a glorious past now down-trodden and oppressed by the minions of an alien race. The glorious past of India also appealed to Disraeli but in a different fashion. It developed in him a lust for an Indian Empire which should surpass in magnificence that of Akbar or of Aurungzebe. Colonies he regarded as encumbrances in that they demanded too great a measure of self-government. But among the subservient Indian peoples he might pursue his autocratic centralizing policy at will. The attitude he adopted towards Afghanistan was only another phase of the policy which led him to proclaim Queen Victoria Empress of India. The consolida-

---

[1] *Afghan Blue Book* (1), 1878, p. 127.

tion of the British dominion in the East was his one great object. In consequence, from the outset of his ministry, the Central Asian question engaged the serious attention of himself and of his Secretary of State for India. They saw quite clearly that some change from the weak and indecisive policy of their predecessors was necessary. They were much less satisfied than those who had gone before them of the innocuous nature of the Russian advance, and were not inclined to regard as meaningless the correspondence then proceeding between Kauffman and Shere Ali. That correspondence, which had had Lord Mayo's approval, was scarcely consistent with Russia's plea that she had no desire to extend her influence across the Oxus. "I hope," wrote Kauffman from Tashkent in the spring of 1873, "that after your death Sirdar Abdullah Jan will make himself an ally and friend of the Emperor[1]." Khiva had fallen, and fallen definitely, in spite of Russia's assurances to the contrary. Russia was also extending her influence in Persia. Thus there was ground for considerable uneasiness with regard to Afghan affairs, and the Home Government wished to take some steps to draw Afghanistan closer to Great Britain. Unfortunately they took the wrong ones. Instead of endeavouring to cajole Shere Ali back

[1] *Central Asia Blue Book*, No. (1), 1881.

to his old allegiance, instead of recognizing that the proper course was to shew him that Great Britain could give him much more than Russia, and that it was to his advantage to fulfil his engagements to her, he was driven still further away by the demand for British agents in Afghanistan. The demand was an ill-timed one, and was founded to a large extent upon a misconception of facts. Now, as in 1868, the minute of an Anglo-Indian official had a very great effect upon the action of the Home Government. To Sir Bartle Frere's representations in 1874 was due Lord Salisbury's despatch to the Governor-General of Jan. 22nd, 1875[1], in which he stated his mistrust of the intelligence forwarded to India by the native Vakil at Kabul, Atta Mahomed Khan, and his desire that a British agency should be established first at Herat and then at Kandahar. As far as Kabul he did not intend to go just yet, recognizing the fanaticism of its inhabitants, but he hoped a mission to that city would come later. It must not be forgotten that when Sir Bartle Frere first mooted the question of an agency at Herat that town was in the possession of Yakub Khan, Shere Ali's insubordinate son. It is doubtful whether Shere Ali heard of Sir Bartle Frere's proposals until his son had again fallen into his hands, but, in any case, the

[1] *Afghan Blue Book* (1), 1878, p. 128.

late proceedings at Herat would not tend to make him any better disposed towards the presence of British agents there.

The misconception in Lord Salisbury's despatch lay in the fact that he stated that at various times the Amir had consented to the presence of British officials at Herat. There was not a word in the Indian archives recording any formal promise on the Amir's part to this effect, and the only evidence that there was such a promise was that of an untrustworthy native spy in the British service, and the conversations of Indian and Afghan officials. Syad Nur Mahomed had certainly mentioned the subject in 1869. But he had regarded it as extremely doubtful whether the Amir would ever consent, and he wished the fact that he had ever suggested such a course kept secret, as, if it leaked out, his life might even be endangered. This was the purport of Lord Northbrook's reply[1], and he also gave the opinions of many eminent Indian officials against Lord Salisbury's proposed measures. The substance of the arguments thus placed before the consideration of the Home Government has already been given[2]. In addition Lord Northbrook said that, though the information furnished by the native Vakil might not be all that could be desired,

---

[1] *Afghan Blue Book* (I), 1878, pp. 129 *et seq.*
[2] Pages 37—40, *supra.*

N.

neither he nor any of his Council had any reason
to regard it as other than fairly full and accurate,
and considered Atta Mahomed as a trustworthy
and intelligent official.   If the Russians advanced
to Merv (the value of which place as a strategic
point was always ridiculously overrated by British
statesmen and the British public at large[1]), then
it might be advisable to enter into more specific
treaty arrangements with the Afghan ruler, and as
a necessary consequence he would be willing to
allow a British agent to be stationed at Herat.   But
it would be most unwise to anticipate the Russian
advance in any way, and until the Russians actually
reached Merv matters might very well remain as
they were.   Lord Northbrook's reasoning did not,
however, appeal to Lord Salisbury.   He thought
that if Merv were occupied the day for an extension of British influence in Afghanistan would have
passed, and in this he was perhaps correct.   But
the demand for the reception of a British mission
at Kabul was hardly the wisest method of attempting to increase that influence.   The mission was to
be at first nominally temporary and directed to
some object of smaller political interest, which the
Governor-General would have no difficulty in finding, or if need be, in creating [2].   This arrangement

---

[1] Curzon, *Russia in Central Asia*, pp. 107, 121.

[2] *Afghan Blue Book* (1), 1878, p. 148.

would only have postponed difficulties, as sooner or later the permanent character of the mission must have become evident and awkward complications have arisen. The better plan both now and at any time during the next two years would have been to state definitely to Russia that there could be no correspondence between Russian officials and the Amir of Afghanistan, and, after thus isolating the latter, to have judiciously enticed him back to friendship with the British. Lord Northbrook reiterated his firm belief that British agents in Afghanistan were impossible, and either because his advice in this particular was neglected, or for the "purely domestic reasons" stated in the letter[1], in which Mr Disraeli offered the Governor-Generalship to Lord Lytton, resigned his office at the beginning of 1876. Although he must share with Lord Mayo and Lord Lytton a good deal of the responsibility for the second Afghan war, in that a different result might have attended the efforts of a greater statesman at Simla in 1873, it is only just to remember that he was much trammelled in his action by the instructions which he received from the Home Government to let matters drift, and that had he been allowed more freedom, he might have succeeded in attaching Shere Ali more firmly to the British alliance. In this was shewn the

[1] Balfour, *Lord Lytton's Indian Administration*, p. 2.

disadvantages of the dual system of Indian Government.   Afghanistan was now also to feel the effects
of the party system.   One party had to rectify the
mistakes of the other and this it endeavoured to
do in a summary but most unsafe manner.   The
Gladstonian Government had sown the wind, the
Conservative Government, largely it must be admitted through its own mismanagement, was to
reap the whirlwind.

CHAPTER IV.

THE SECOND AFGHAN WAR (1876—1880).

Lord Lytton.—Instructions from the Home Government.—The
Afghan-Russian correspondence.—Demand for a British mis-
sion at Kabul.—Shere Ali's refusal.—Renewal of the demand.
—Atta Mahomed at Simla.—Occupation of Quetta.—The
Peshawar Conference.—Atta Mahomed withdrawn from Kabul.
—Arrival of a Russian mission at Kabul.—Renewed demand
for the reception of a British mission.—The Ali Masjid incident.
—Shere Ali's correspondence with Kauffman and Stolietoff.—
The Second Afghan War.—Death of Shere Ali.—Succession
of Yakub Khan.—Treaty of Gandamak.—Massacre of Cavagnari's mission.—Second phase of the War.—Abdication
of Yakub Khan.—Difficulties as to his successor.—Separation
of Kandahar from Kabul.

LORD NORTHBROOK was succeeded by Lord
Lytton, perhaps the most abused man in Indian
history. Other politicians, Macaulay, Sir Charles
Metcalfe or Sir Courtenay Ilbert for example, have
fallen foul of some section or other of British or
Indian opinion and have been made to feel what
party rancour can do. But Lord Lytton was the
vehicle for carrying out a policy which a large section
of the British public loathed, and his comparative

failure subjected him to the taunts of an ever-increasing and ultimately victorious party. Lord Auckland's folly was infinitely greater, and his failure infinitely more disastrous than Lord Lytton's, but the Press was not such a powerful instrument in 1842 as in 1882 and communication with India was longer and more laborious. Yet it is a mistake to regard Lord Lytton as a visionary[1], or to maintain that his merits as a poet and dramatist prevented his possessing any as a politician. His administration of India in time of famine with an important war on hand is a complete answer to the charge that he was destitute of statesmanlike qualities. Perhaps his beautifully worded and magnificently expressed but desperately lengthy despatches—embellished with many quotations from the poets whom he knew so well, but who were not probably quite so familiar to the statesmen to whom the despatches were addressed—have done as much as anything else to conceal his real abilities. Like Warren Hastings he seemed to possess the gift of writing a long state paper upon anything or nothing. His policy towards Afghanistan was the weakest part of his administration. He knew exactly what he wanted and had made up his mind that closer relations between England and Afghanistan were necessary, and in

[1] Hanna, *Second Afghan War, passim.*

this he was quite correct. But he adopted the wrong means to the attainment of his object. That could, he thought, be brought about in one way and in one way only, and in this lay his cardinal error. For this he is not altogether to be blamed. He knew singularly little of India when he started to govern it, and his opportunities for independent study were limited by the fact that he was chosen to be the instrument for executing a policy preconceived by his political leaders. His naturally impulsive nature did the rest. He hoped at the outset to obtain his object by diplomacy, but his diplomacy was not exactly of the order calculated to reassure such a suspicious mind as that of Shere Ali. There was too much of the iron hand and too little of the velvet glove about it. Its failure led Lytton to other and much more far-reaching schemes, which must be considered in their place. Nevertheless, although he failed, and although it was almost inevitable that he should fail, he did much both for India and Afghanistan. His acceptance of Abdur Rahman Khan as Amir, even admitting that it was forced upon him by circumstances, is some reparation for a multitude of other blunders, and the twenty years of peace and prosperity which that selection gave Afghanistan have done much to obliterate the memory of the three years which preceded them.

Lord Lytton was given a very free hand by his leaders. His instructions[1] manifest a strong desire on the part of the Home Government to obtain the friendship and good will of the Amir, subject only to the condition that a British mission should be admitted into Afghanistan. All Shere Ali's demands of 1869 were considered in a conciliatory spirit. The Governor-General was to deal with the question of a fixed and augmented subsidy as the circumstances and the attitude of the Amir might dictate. He was empowered to recognize Abdullah Jan as heir to the throne of Afghanistan, and to give the Amir much more explicit assurances of aid in case of unprovoked aggression, right of judgment as to the circumstances which caused it being of course retained. But over all hung the condition which made every effort of no avail.

Meanwhile the correspondence between Kauffman and Shere Ali was still proceeding. The marriage of the Duke of Edinburgh, the acknowledgment of Abdullah Jan, the fall of Khokand, were made the subject of epistolary communication. It cannot be said that Shere Ali displayed any effusive delight at the receipt of the Russian letters, or upon the arrival of the Russian native envoys, the first of whom reached Kabul in the first week of September, 1875. From the corre-

[1] Balfour, *Lord Lytton's Indian Administration*, pp. 88 *et seq.*

spondence itself it would appear that Shere Ali
was more sinned against than sinning, and that,
though the growing frequency of the letters between him and the Russians might afford the Home
Government good ground for uneasiness, the Russian and not the Afghan Government was the real
offender and should have been called to account. But
the action of the British ministry at this time was
hampered by events proceeding in South-Eastern
Europe, and the general unrest prevalent in European politics probably made it desirous of bringing
its influence to bear upon Afghanistan rather than
upon Russia.

Lord Lytton had no difficulty in discovering a
matter of smaller political interest to which his
mission might be directed. It came readily to
hand in the shape of his own accession to office
and the impending assumption by the Queen of the
title of Empress of India. Soon after his arrival
in India, he wrote to the Amir to inform him that
Sir Lewis Pelly would be the head of a special
mission to Kabul to announce to him these new
arrangements[1]. Such a mission had at least European precedents in the special embassies sent to
other courts to announce the accession of a new
sovereign. Shere Ali replied in a characteristic
letter. He could write in plain and straightforward

---

[1] *Afghan Blue Book* (1), 1878, p. 174.

language when he chose, as he had shewn Lord
Northbrook several times, but on this occasion he
allowed himself to run riot in clouds of Oriental
verbiage and compliment.   Nevertheless, although
Lord Lytton complained of the studied ambiguity
of the letter[1], in reality its purport was quite clear.
Shere Ali would have none of the proposed mission.
The recent announcement, through the Commissioner of Peshawar, of Lord Lytton's accession and
the proposed addition to the Queen's titles, was
quite enough, and the results of the Simla Conference were "sufficient and efficient for the exalta-
tion and permanence of friendly relations between
India and Afghanistan."   If there were any new
matters concerning which the British Government
desired discussion, he would send a confidential
agent to India[2].

Such was the tenour of a reply which was
equivalent to a direct refusal.   It was further am-
plified by a letter received from the British native
agent at Kabul, who stated that the Amir had three
great reasons for declining to receive the proposed
mission.   In the first place he would have the ut-
most difficulty in protecting it against the fanaticism of the inhabitants.   That this was a very
real difficulty after-events were only too terribly to

[1] *Afghan Blue Book* (1), 1878, p. 167.
[2] *Ibid.*, pp. 174, 175.

shew. Secondly, if the British envoy "should put
forward any such weighty matter of state that its
entertainment by His Highness in view of the
demands of the time should prove difficult and he
should verbally reject it, there would occur a breach
of the friendship of the two Governments." Finally
if the British demanded an envoy Russia would
demand one as well[1]. In his last reason Shere Ali
touched a very weak spot. This was the legacy
left Lord Lytton by his predecessors. Shere Ali
had no reason to think other than he did. In
spite of the assurances of the British and Russian
Governments in 1872 and 1873, he had been encouraged by Lord Mayo to receive communications
from the Russian Governor of the nearest province,
and if the Russians sent letters, there was no reason
why they should not send an envoy as well. The
Russian advance had filled him with alarm, and it
must have seemed to him that the Russians were
more to be feared than the British, who did nothing
to stop them, although Russia had declared to Great
Britain her intention of proceeding no further in
Central Asia.

Lord Lytton, feeling that Shere Ali's refusal
could not be accepted with dignity by the British
Government nor passed over in silence, determined
to give the recalcitrant Amir another chance. A

[1] *Afghan Blue Book* (1), 1878, p. 175.

second letter was addressed to him which presumed that his declaration of inability to accept a mission was founded on a misconception of the Governor-General's objects, and informed him that by rejecting the hand of friendship now frankly held out to him, he was compelling the British Government to regard Afghanistan as a state which had voluntarily isolated itself from its alliance and support[1]. Atta Mahomed, our native agent, was at the same time instructed to inform Shere Ali that no difficulty need present itself to him with regard to Russia, as the Government of the Czar had given the British Government written pledges not to interfere, directly or indirectly, at any time in the affairs of Afghanistan. The reference is, of course, to the Granville-Gortschakoff agreement, which scarcely had the significance of a formal treaty and of which, in any case, the Russo-Afghan correspondence was a distinct breach. Atta Mahomed was to reiterate and amplify the warnings contained in the Governor-General's letter to the Amir[2].

It is only just to relate that three members of the Governor's Council, Sir William Muir, Sir Henry Norman, and Sir Arthur Hobhouse, dissented from the views of Lord Lytton and the majority of their colleagues. They held that the Amir was quite

[1] *Afghan Blue Book* (1), 1878, p. 176.
[2] *Ibid.*, p. 177.

justified by the treaties of 1855 and 1857 in refusing to receive a British mission, and indeed this
was so. However desirable such a mission might
be, Lord Lytton's way was hardly the right way in
which to obtain it. The exact extent of Russian
influence at Kabul at this particular moment will
always remain doubtful. That it was considerable
in 1878 is certain[1], but it is hardly fair to compare
1876 with 1878, as much had happened in the in-
terval. But even allowing that it was much greater
than in all probability was actually the case, persuasion, and not threats, would have been the best
method by which to approach Shere Ali. Had the
concessions which, at the commencement of his
tenure of office, Lord Lytton was authorised to
make, been offered Shere Ali without the condition he so much disliked, they would have
convinced him that he had more to gain from
Great Britain than from Russia, and he would
have honestly endeavoured to receive a mission
if such a course had been possible to him.

Shere Ali did not answer Lord Lytton's letter
for two months. The lengthy delay seemed to
the Governor-General to imply studied discourtesy.
Probably this was not intended. The wheels of
the official chariot move on occasion as slowly in
semi-barbarous states as they do in those which

[1] Roberts, *Forty-one Years in India*, pp. 421, 558.

have pretensions to civilization, and the matter was a difficult one. Shere Ali was as fixed in his determination not to receive a mission as Lord Lytton to send one, and the former could for the present see no way out of his difficulties. His intrigues with Russia may have begun in real earnest from this date. The tension with Great Britain would make him better disposed towards his other near neighbour, whilst Russia, foreseeing complications in Europe, would not be unwilling to utilise every available opportunity of obtaining a foothold in Afghanistan.

Of the three suggestions contained in Shere Ali's letter, obviously intended to delay, if not to avoid altogether, the acceptance of the proposed mission, the third was adopted, and Atta Mahomed was sent to Simla, which he reached on Oct. 6th, 1876. He related in detail Shere Ali's grievances, adding little that was new. The most important were Lord Northbrook's interference on behalf of his son Yakub, the Sistan boundary award, presents forwarded directly by Lord Northbrook to his vassal the Mir of Wakkan, the repeated rejections of his requests for an offensive and defensive alliance and the formal acknowledgment of Abdullah Jan as his successor[1]. These are all that are given in the Governor-General's

---

[1] *Afghan Blue Book* (1), 1878, pp. 167 and 180.

very lengthy despatch of May 10th, 1877, but there were others almost as important, for example the treatment of Syad Nur Mahomed, who had left Simla at the close of the conference in 1873 in high dudgeon at a supposed insult from British officials, and whose influence had since been directed entirely against the British[1]. Atta Mahomed also gave the Governor-General his views on the general position of affairs in Afghanistan, and expressed his opinion that the Amir regarded the Russian native agent as a source of great embarrassment.

As the outcome of the meeting, the agent was sent back to Kabul with power to accede to the Amir's wishes with regard to the succession and the treaty of alliance, conditionally on his receiving British agents at Herat and other places on the frontier. Lord Lytton was willing to postpone sending them until the treaty of alliance had been signed, and this would certainly have been a wise move, had there ever been any prospect that Shere Ali would receive British envoys anywhere in his dominions. To an agent at Herat there was not quite so much objection as to one at Kabul, for the people of Herat are a mixed race and lack the fanaticism displayed by their more eastern brethren. Shere Ali was, no doubt, equally averse

[1] *Afghan Blue Book* (1), 1878, p. 181.

to the presence of a British agent anywhere in his dominions, and he must have known the true facts of the case, namely that the establishment of an agency at Herat would be followed by a demand for a similar one at Kandahar, and afterwards at Kabul. The treaty which Atta Mahomed was empowered to make was to embody the above concessions, and was in addition to open up Afghanistan to British subjects wishing to trade, and to provide for the safety of certain trade routes[1].

Atta Mahomed reached Kabul towards the end of October and immediately presented the Governor-General's letter to the Amir. He heard nothing concerning it for a month. Meanwhile political relations in Europe were becoming strained, and there was considerable tension between Great Britain and Russia over the South-Eastern European question. Of this Shere Ali was probably aware, and it may have seemed to him a means of extricating himself from his difficulties. By temporizing he might save himself, for in the event of war between Great Britain and Russia the former power would be too much occupied to trouble about Afghanistan.

During the last three months of 1876 an important step was taken with regard to Indian

[1] *Afghan Blue Book* (1), 1878, p. 190.

frontier defence. The occupation of Quetta—-
recommended by General Jacob, administrator
of the Sind frontier, and approved both by his
successor, Sir Henry Green, and by Sir Henry
Rawlinson—was at last carried out. As in the
case of many other of Lord Lytton's acts, opinions
differed very much with regard to its wisdom at
the time. But, on the whole, in spite of the fact
that it added greatly to Shere Ali's growing mistrust, it must be considered most prudent. Whilst
the occupation of Quetta was originally regarded
somewhat in the light of a temporary expedient,
no Government since 1876 has ever seriously considered its evacuation. Its occupation was carried
out without any difficulty or bloodshed and was
the result of a pacific arrangement with the
Khan of Khelat. Quetta occupies a position of
extraordinary natural strength as well as of
great strategic importance, for it dominates every
line of advance on Sind and all roads south of
Herat lead to it. The significance of its occupation, however, in the present connexion, lies in
the fact that it caused grave displeasure to Shere
Ali.

To return to Afghanistan. At a Durbar held
on November 23rd, 1876, the gist of a desultory
discussion was that the Afghan Government was
not in a position to receive British officers. The

discussion was protracted throughout the month of December, and the final outcome of it was a report from the British agent to the Commissioner of Peshawar, through whose hands all his correspondence with the Indian Government passed, to the effect that Shere Ali proposed sending his Prime Minister, Syad Nur Mahomed, and the Master of the Horse (Mir Akhor), Ahmad Shah, to meet a British envoy at Peshawar or some other place on the frontier. He added that the Durbar authorities intended imposing very stringent conditions if they gave their consent to the admission of a British envoy. In view of the past and present of Afghanistan these restrictions were very fairly reasonable, and would have afforded a sound basis for further negotiation. The Afghan Government was not to be responsible for any accident to the life or property of a British officer. The duties of the British officers were to be fully defined, and they were not to meddle in the internal affairs of Afghanistan. Should a Russian envoy come to Kabul in spite of the wishes of the British Government, the latter was to make its own arrangements for preventing his arrival. The last article is very indefinite. As it reads it may be interpreted that, if the British Government did not offer sufficient assistance to Afghanistan, the latter might decline any assistance at all while still permitting the

residence of British officers. A closer study of
the original Persian would be interesting, as it
might (not improbably) reveal the fact that a
negative has been omitted, and the real meaning
was that the Kabul Government would decline
to admit British officers if it were not satisfied
with the assistance offered by the British Government[1].

Syad Nur Mahomed met Sir Lewis Pelly at
Peshawar on January 30th, 1877. He was hardly
the best envoy the Amir could have chosen, for
since 1873 he had not been well disposed towards
the British. The questions under consideration
were too delicate to be handled by two such
agents as himself and Sir Lewis Pelly. It is not
necessary to enter into a lengthy discussion of
the proceedings which took place at Peshawar.
Lord Lytton has been accused of every kind of
misrepresentation, short of downright lying, both
with regard to his instructions to Sir Lewis Pelly
and the letter in which he authorised the latter to
close the conference[2]. There was, however, much
that was just, as well as much that was untenable,
in his position. Having once convinced himself
that agents at Herat were absolutely necessary,
and that such a solution of the present difficulties

[1] *Afghan Blue Book* (1), 1878, pp. 192 *et seq.*
[2] Hanna, *Second Afghan War*, Chapter VII.

was the only one, it was a very easy step to persuade himself of the absolute justice of his demands and of Shere Ali's insensate folly in refusing them. Nevertheless, his contention that Shere Ali, by sending Syad Nur Mahomed to Peshawar, had ceded the preliminary basis of negotiations seems a fair one. He had laid that condition down as essential to any further steps. Therefore when it became evident that Syad Nur Mahomed had no authority to grant this preliminary condition and that he was merely fencing in order to gain time, Lord Lytton was quite justified in declaring that there was nothing left to negotiate about, and that there was no reason why the Afghan envoy should not immediately return to Kabul. With the rest of the Governor-General's letter to Sir Lewis Pelly we have here little concern. Satisfied of the necessity of British agents at Herat and elsewhere, Lord Lytton tried to make out just and sufficient reasons why they should be there, but the attempt is not very convincing, and the endeavour to whittle down British obligations to Afghanistan to those embodied in the treaties of 1855 and 1857 is decidedly unfortunate[1].

---

[1] For the proceedings of the Peshawar Conference and the Governor-General's letter to Sir Lewis Pelly, see *Afghan Blue Book* (1), 1878, pp. 196—214.

Up to this point the conference had had no effect. It had so far produced a reiteration of Shere Ali's grievances and a re-statement of the Governor-General's position. In both cases there were some additions but no common basis for negotiation had as yet been discovered. The course of events was hastened by Syad Nur Mahomed's death on March 26th, which was a great blow to Shere Ali. The surviving envoy, the Mir Akhor, declared that he had no authority from Kabul to answer any question from the British Government and so Sir Lewis Pelly was instructed by the Governor-General to declare the conference at an end[1]. Shere Ali had meanwhile despatched another envoy to Peshawar who had, it was reported, full powers to grant the necessary preliminary condition; but in spite of this, the conference was closed by Lord Lytton "to avoid further entanglement[2]." In so doing he committed an error. It is quite probable that the new agent had no more definite instructions than the old one, and was only sent to procrastinate; but still Lord Lytton would have greatly strengthened his position by waiting to discover how far he was authorised to make concessions. He had, however, by this time become thoroughly convinced of the

[1] *Afghan Blue Book* (1), 1878, p. 170.
[2] *Ibid.*, p. 191.

Amir's disaffection and of his leaning towards an alliance with Russia. He himself had done much by his demands for British agents in Afghanistan to drive Shere Ali into the arms of Russia, but the evidence furnished by the *Afghan Blue Book* to shew how deeply Shere Ali was involved is not particularly convincing. It consists of two extracts, one from the Kandahar news letter, which gives information furnished by a nameless Kandahari—a mule-driver—with regard to Shere Ali's communications with the Russian agent[1], and one from the diary of Syud Ahmad, Atta Mahomed's assistant, who was at this time in charge of the British embassy, which declared that the Amir had ceased to talk Jehad (sacred war) openly, but was none the less making preparations for it[2]. This is hardly sufficient matter on which to found so grave a charge. There may, of course, have been other considerations which led Lord Lytton to act as he did which are not available for the examination of the outsider, for even in blue-books we cannot expect to find a complete record of all that has taken place. But judging from the material we have at hand, Lord Lytton would have done well to wait. Impulsiveness and impatience seem however to have been his most noteworthy charac-

[1] *Afghan Blue Book* (1), 1878, p. 178.
[2] *Ibid.*, p. 221.

teristics in connexion with Afghan diplomacy. He
never realized quite fully the force of the Oriental
doctrine that Time is Naught, and that it is un-
dignified to hurry. In consequence he shewed
his hand much too soon and much too openly.
Concessions, however small, should have come
first, demands afterwards. Such was the only way
to convince Shere Ali, suspiciou; and resentful by
nature and shackled by the one-sided treaty of
1855, that the British Government was acting in
good faith. Lord Lytton's task was, in any case,
an extremely difficult one and needed statesmanship of the highest order, and he must not therefore
be too severely censured for his failure. In history
we can only see one course. Could two courses
be adopted and worked side by side, comparison
would be easy. As it is, we can only compare
what has been done with a fabric of our own
imagination, and in the last resort can only say
that someone else would have done differently
and have done better, an extremely unsatisfactory
conclusion.

Our native agent at Kabul was now finally
withdrawn. The statement that he was worse
than useless, and was but a tool in the Amir's
hands[1], accords but ill with the substantial present
of 10,000 rupees the Governor-General had given

[1] Balfour, *Lord Lytton's Indian Administration*, p. 160.

him after the Simla Conference in consideration of
his valuable services to the British Government.
The difficulties of his position have been already
enumerated and there is no reason to believe that
he was less successful than any other Mohammedan
would have been in his place. His withdrawal
implied an absolute cleavage from Afghanistan
and was a definite declaration that all future advances must come from Shere Ali. Whether, in
view of Russia's forward movement in Central
Asia, Lord Lytton acted quite wisely in thus
cutting himself off from all communication with
Afghanistan at this juncture is open to question,
though it is difficult to see what other course he
could have adopted consistently with his previous
statements. All the information he desired he
hoped to obtain through Cavagnari, who was now
appointed Deputy Commissioner of Peshawar.

For several months no communications passed
between the Courts of Simla and Kabul. Lord
Salisbury welcomed the conclusion of the Peshawar
Conference as clearly defining the relations between
the British Government and that of Afghanistan,
but was careful to add that if Shere Ali made any
advances within a reasonable time, they were not
to be rejected[1].

Lord Lytton proceeded to occupy the leisure

---

[1] *Afghan Blue Book* (1), 1878, p. 224.

given him by the cessation of relations with
Afghanistan in a new scheme of frontier re-
organization. He wished to create a separate
Trans-Indus province, to be military in nature
and under the Chief Commissionership of an able
and experienced officer. The first Chief Commissioner was to be Sir Frederick Roberts. But his
plans were destined to be executed by others at a
later date, and he had only established a frontier
agency at Gilgit when his schemes were rudely
interrupted by the news that a Russian mission
had reached Kabul. War had broken out between Russia and Turkey in April, 1877, and in
January, 1878, the Russians had crossed the
Balkans. Disraeli had given Russia a significant
hint by bringing Indian troops to Malta, that
Great Britain might find armed intervention necessary, and the Russian mission to Kabul seems to
have been intended as a counterblast. It appears
to have started from Tashkent on June 13th, the
first day of the Congress of Berlin, and to have
reached Kabul on July 22nd. Its head was
General Stolietoff, though Cavagnari had reported
that General Abrahamoff, Governor of Samarcand,
was in charge[1]. The treaty, which had put an
end to the fear of war between Great Britain and
Russia, had been signed on July 13th, nine days

[1] *Afghan Blue Book* (1), 1878, p. 228.

before the mission arrived at Kabul, though news of it probably did not reach Stolietoff for some weeks. There is no evidence to shew that Shere Ali was any more anxious to receive the Russian mission than he had been to receive the English one. He adopted the same course of action with regard to both, urged the same objections to Kauffman as he had to Lord Lytton, and was as desirous of temporizing by sending a minister to Tashkent as he had been by sending Syad Nur Mahomed to Peshawar. But Kauffman would hear of no refusal, and the mission proceeded on its way, and by so doing placed Shere Ali in a most unenviable position. What he had so long sought to avoid—a definite choice between the two great neighbouring Empires—was now thrust upon him. Up to the signature of the Berlin treaty the tension between Great Britain and Russia might have enabled him to make his own terms, but all hopes in that direction were now at an end, and whilst pride and policy dictated an honourable reception of the Russian embassy, he must have felt that such a reception would only bring down upon him the wrath of the British Government.

Lord Lytton and the British Government also stood at the parting of the ways. Two courses of action lay open to them. In the one case they might exert pressure on Afghanistan, in the

other, upon Russia. The latter course would, undoubtedly, have been the more just. A Russian
mission to Afghanistan was an unfriendly act
planned and undertaken when Russia was pre-
paring for hostilities with Great Britain. Peace
had been established between the two powers
and therefore the British Government should have
demanded the instant withdrawal of the mission,
with an apology for its presence. That Russia
would have immediately assented is shewn by
the haste in which Stolietoff left Kabul when he
heard of possible war between Great Britain and
Afghanistan. Accounts with Shere Ali could have
been settled afterwards, and Lord Lytton would
have, this time, held a commanding position. For
the Amir had shewn that the envoys of a foreign
and a European power could be received with
perfect safety in his capital, and though he might
plead that Russia's connexions with Afghanistan
in the past had not, like those of England, left
unpleasant memories behind them, he could hardly
expect such an excuse to be taken seriously. But,
in any event, it could not be denied that Russia
had forced the mission upon him, and therefore
Russia ought to be required to explain its presence.
What is just in politics is not however always expedient and it is much easier and safer to threaten
a weak state than a strong one. It is of course

quite possible that the result in either case would have been the same, and that had Russia been approached first, and been compelled to assent to the withdrawal of her mission, Shere Ali would still have forbidden a British embassy to enter his territories.   But if this had happened he would have been deprived of his last standing ground, and all right would have passed to Lord Lytton's side. Such a method of procedure was, unfortunately, quite foreign to the Governor-General's impulsive diplomacy.   More convinced than ever, if possible, of Shere Ali's hostility and duplicity, he sought the earliest opportunity to persuade others of it also.   He therefore proposed to send a mission to Kabul at once, with Sir Neville Chamberlain at its head.   Three courses of action and three only were in his opinion still feasible : such an alliance with the Amir as would effectually exclude Russian influence, to break up the Afghan kingdom and to put in its place a sovereign more friendly to our interests and dependent on our support, or to conquer and hold as much of Afghan territory as was necessary to the safety of the North-West frontier[1].   These methods he put in order of merit and the last was in his opinion very much the worst.   It will be considered more fully hereafter in connexion with the future of Afghanistan.

[1] Balfour, *Lord Lytton's Indian Administration*, p. 255.

The second was little, if at all, wiser. It implied, as
Lord Lytton explained more fully later, the complete disintegration of Afghanistan. An Afghanistan of small kingdoms, however dependent on the
support of the British and well-affected towards
them, would prove of little service in stemming a
Russian advance. Any united action would be
impossible. Opportunities for Russian intrigues,
for intestine disputes in each separate kingdom,
and for quarrels between the kingdoms themselves,
would be multiplied tenfold, and the fact that the
British Government had dismembered their state
would not tend to increase any love the Afghans
might bear it. The policy of a divided Afghanistan has been tried and has failed, and the first
of Lord Lytton's suggestions has been proved to
deserve the place he gave it in his list.

On the 14th of August, 1878, the Governor-
General despatched a letter to Shere Ali demanding
the immediate reception of a British mission[1]. On
the 17th, Abdullah Jan, Shere Ali's favourite son
and heir-apparent—for whose sake he had made
Yakub Khan a prisoner and Ayub Khan an exile—
died. This untoward event threw Shere Ali into
one of those states bordering on madness to which
his unbalanced nature was subject, and rendered
him for a while incapable of business. Lord Lytton

[1] *Afghan Blue Book* (1), 1878, p. 232.

thereupon delayed the departure of the British envoy until August 30th[1]. This envoy, a native, was sent to announce to the Amir the forthcoming departure of the British mission, which was to start on September 16th, whether he had or had not by that time been received by the Amir. The emissary chosen for this purpose, Ghulam Hassan Khan by name, was certainly not the most suitable, as he had been withdrawn in 1864 for intriguing with Azim Khan against Shere Ali. The delay thus allowed by Lord Lytton was perhaps not sufficient to enable Shere Ali to recover his mental balance, but Lord Lytton declined to sanction any further extension of time on the ground that Shere Ali was only procrastinating in the hope of obtaining some definite settlement with Russia. Stolietoff had left Kabul on August 24th, when he heard of the proposed British mission, leaving behind him advice to the Amir to keep it out at all costs. Could its exact date be determined, the treaty said to have been made by him with Shere Ali, and written from memory for Sir Frederick Roberts[2] by Mirza Mahomed Khan, would furnish more trustworthy evidence to shew how deeply Shere Ali was implicated at this juncture. But it is quite conceivable that he had by this time realized

[1] *Afghan Blue Book* (1), 1878, p. 234.
[2] Roberts, *Forty-one Years in India*, Appendix VII. pp. 562 et seq.

that, owing to his reception of a Russian envoy, Russia had won the race and that he had no more to hope from Great Britain. It behoved him then to make as close an alliance as possible with his new friends. The terms of this treaty very closely resembled those offered by Lord Lytton to Shere Ali at various times save that there was no stipulation with regard to the obnoxious permanent mission. The correspondence discovered by Sir Frederick Roberts began soon after Stolietoff had left Kabul.

Ghulam Hassan Khan was received by the Amir on September 12th. He described the Afghan ruler as being in a very bad humour as the result of his difficulties, but thought it probable that he would yield to superior force and admit the British after he had got rid of the Russians.

Sir Neville Chamberlain, the head of the proposed mission, reached Peshawar on September 12th. With his instructions we are not called upon to deal as they were never in the slightest danger of being carried out. But Lord Lytton had shewn a great deal more wisdom in this selection than in that of many other of his agents, and Chamberlain, had he ever reached Kabul, might in consequence of his conciliatory disposition and his known dislike of the ultra-

Forward policy have persuaded Shere Ali to accept the "preliminary condition," and to admit and to do his best to secure the safety of British agents at Balkh and Herat, whilst loathing their presence. But Sir Neville never reached the Afghan capital. Wearied of Shere Ali's persistent delays, the Governor-General ordered the mission to advance at once. A detachment of it under Cavagnari was prevented by Faiz Mahomed from entering the Khyber Pass.

In the course of an interview between himself and Cavagnari, conducted with perfect courtesy on both sides, the Afghan officer informed the latter that his desire to act in a perfectly friendly manner was being shewn by the fact that he had consented to a meeting and had restrained his soldiers from firing on the British troops. He had, however, received no orders to permit the mission to enter the Khyber Pass, and without such orders he could not allow it to proceed. If the mission would wait, he would communicate with Kabul and ask for instructions. Cavagnari replied that he had no authority to agree to further delay and begged Faiz Mahomed not to take upon himself the responsibility of stopping the mission. The Afghan could only repeat his orders, and as he began to comment with some heat upon the British dealings with the Afridis, Cavagnari thought it best to close the

interview by a final question as to whether the
passage of the mission would be opposed by force.
The Governor of Ali Masjid replied that it would,
and that Cavagnari might take it as kindness and
because he remembered friendship that he did not
fire upon the British for what they had done
already[1]. The British officers thereupon shook
hands with him, mounted their horses and returned
to the main body. Cavagnari fully admitted in
his report of the meeting the courtesy of the
Afghan Governor, which had, in his opinion, prevented a collision that would have proved fatal
to the small British party.

The use which Lord Lytton made of this incident bears a striking resemblance to that to
which Bismarck had turned a still more famous
incident some ten years before. At Ems, in 1870,
the King of Prussia informed Benedetti, the French
Ambassador, in a perfectly friendly manner that
he could add nothing to the statement he had
made at their recent meeting with regard to the
impossibility of the Prussian Government giving
the French a formal guarantee that it would never
in the future support the claims of a Hohenzollern
candidate to the throne of Spain. There was, therefore, no need for a second interview with regard
to that subject. As at Ali Masjid, the refusal was

[1] *Afghan Blue Book* (1), 1878, p. 251.

couched in courteous language and contained in itself nothing which might not have been made the subject of further diplomatic negotiation. But in each case a scheming statesman was supplied with a pretext, for which he had long wished, for bringing about a war he eagerly desired. A comparatively harmless incident was, by a dexterous concealment of material facts, magnified into an important rebuff, the only possible way of avenging which was by war.

In order to avenge the affront thus sustained Lord Lytton was in favour of immediate military measures, but the hands of the too hasty Governor-General were stayed by the Home Government, which declared that Shere Ali must be given another opportunity for repentance. With a view to this an ultimatum was despatched on Nov. 2nd, demanding an apology in writing on or before Nov. 20th for the repulse of the mission at Ali Masjid and the permanent reception of a British mission. In the event of an unfavourable reply or of no reply at all, military operations would be commenced on Nov. 21st. No answer to Lord Lytton's ultimatum arrived until Nov. 30th, when Cavagnari received one dated Nov. 19th. He was however of the opinion that the letter had been written by the Amir after the fall of Ali Masjid and was a substitute for one earlier in date and haughtier in

tone[1]. But the reply, even had it been received
prior to Nov. 20th, would not have been deemed
satisfactory, as it contained no apology for the
treatment of the mission and declined to permit
anything but a temporary mission, the numbers of
which were to be dictated by Shere Ali himself.
No stop was put, therefore, to the military
operations.

Soon after leaving Kabul Stolietoff had written
from Tashkent to the Amir's foreign minister ex-
pressing a hope that those who wished to enter
Kabul from the east would find the gate closed.
On Oct. 8th he wrote again from the Emperor's
court in Livadia to the effect that he was busy day
and night in the Amir's service, and that, thank
God, his labours had not been without avail[2]. But
the result was not very obvious, as in response
to Shere Ali's direct appeal to the Emperor
Alexander II. for assistance, he was roughly told
by Kauffman to make peace with the British, if
they gave him the chance[3]. On Nov. 26th
Kauffman wrote to General Raznogoff, who was
still at Kabul, notwithstanding the fact that
hostilities had broken out, advising him to leave
Kabul at once and to shew the Amir how

[1] Balfour, *Lord Lytton's Indian Administration*, p. 304.

[2] *Central Asia Blue Book* (1), 1881, p. 18. Balfour, *Lord Lytton's Indian Administration*, p. 307.

[3] *Central Asia Blue Book*, *ib.*, p. 19.

impossible it was for Russia to assist him in winter.

At the same time Shere Ali was informed that the British ministers had given a pledge to the Czar not to interfere with the independence of Afghanistan[1]. It is possible, therefore, that Russia had been mediating in London on behalf of the unhappy prince whom she had brought into such serious trouble. Shere Ali renewed his appeal on Dec. 8th on the ground of the recent alliance concluded through General Stolietoff on behalf of his Imperial Majesty, and asked for 32,000 troops[2]. He left Kabul on Dec. 13th before receiving an answer, declaring that he would lay his case before the Czar. The cause and purpose of his departure were explained in a firman of Dec. 22nd, in which he declared to his subjects that it was the Emperor's desire that the British should not be admitted into the country and should be treated with deceit and deception until the cold season had passed away, when the Russian Government, having repeated the Bismillah, the Bismillah would come to the assistance of Afghanistan. The Bismillah might, but the Russian Government, which had probably never expected that matters would come to the arbitrament of war, had no intention of so doing,

---

[1] *Central Asia Blue Book* (1), 1881, pp. 19 *et seq.*

[2] Roberts, *Forty-one Years in India*, p. 560.

and in Jan., 1879, definitely declined to assist the
Amir. He was dissuaded from continuing his
journey to Petersburg and was advised to make
peace with the British and return to Afghanistan.
He died, however, at Mazar-i-Sharif on Feb. 21st,
having realized at last that during the last few
years of his rule he had been nothing more than a
Russian cat's-paw, one of those agents who could so
easily be thrown over by Russia when they had
answered her purpose. He had once bitterly complained that the friendship of the British was a
word written on ice, before his death he was to
discover to his cost that that of the Russians was
a word written on water. By his dealings with
Russia he had gained nothing and had brought
upon himself a war, which, whatever its end, was
bound to be of service to that country in that it
weakened two possible sources of danger, Afghanistan and India. But in truth Russia was more to
blame than he, and a less impatient statesman and
a better judge of character than Lord Lytton might
have been able to warn him of the dangers of a
Russian alliance and to cajole him back to his
English allegiance. Shere Ali had little of that
shrewdness and worldly wisdom possessed by his
great successor, Abdur Rahman, who was careful
never to commit himself, and to be always, if
possible, on the winning side.

Shere Ali's death brought about of necessity a re-construction of the British plans. Lord Lytton was now of the opinion that a disintegrated Afghanistan was the best for British purposes[1], but was still willing to persevere in an attempt to carry out the programme of a strong united and independent kingdom, in which of course British agents were to be resident. For the execution of this plan it was necessary to find some successor to Shere Ali, to whom the government might be handed over. This successor seemed to be present in the person of Yakub Khan, the late Amir's eldest son, who reported his father's death to the British Government—now in practical military command of Afghanistan—with an intimation that he was desirous of its friend-ship. Yakub had been active and energetic in his youth but the long imprisonment he had suffered at the hands of his father, and from which he had only been released to take up the reins of government when the latter departed for Petersburg, had done much to stamp out his finer qualities. His letter was suitably acknowledged, and he was informed of the terms on which the British Government was willing to make peace. These were the renunciation by the new Amir of all authority over the Khyber and Micheri Passes and the independent frontier tribes and the cession of Kuram, Pishin, and Sibi to

---

[1] Balfour, *Lord Lytton's Indian Administration*, p. 310.

the British. The foreign affairs of Afghanistan
were to be conducted in accordance with the advice
and wishes of the British Government and British
officers were to be accredited to Kabul[1]. To the
two last conditions Yakub readily assented. He
knew that they had formed the bone of contention
between his father and the British, and probably
thought that by granting the demand for a British
mission at Kabul he would save himself from what
he disliked still more, the cession of territory. And
he must have been fully aware that by refusing
these last demands he would be throwing away
all chances of the succession, which would, in that
case, be offered to some more pliant candidate,
claimants to the throne of Kabul being always
very plentiful. His efforts were however of no
avail, and the territorial concessions were insisted
upon. Yakub was thereupon compelled to yield, and
did so with as good a grace as possible, and, after
some delay, the Treaty of Gandamak was signed
on May 26th, 1879. This, the most formal engagement ever entered into with Afghanistan, must
have seemed to Lord Lytton the crown and con-
summation of his policy, as it embodied all, or
almost all, for which he had striven. And indeed,
if it had been kept, the judgment we are compelled
to pass upon that policy would be different, as,

---

[1] *Afghan Blue Book* (5), 1881.

however much the second Afghan war might be thought avoidable, Lord Lytton's work would at least have the approval which is merited by success however attained. The Treaty of Gandamak contained, in addition to the four conditions mentioned above, articles under which Yakub Khan was to be supported with money, arms and troops against any foreign aggression which might result from his connexion with Great Britain, engaged to place no hindrances in the way of the extension of trade and telegraphs, and was to have an annual subsidy of six lakhs of rupees[1]. The Amir left Gandamak apparently well satisfied, and Lord Lytton prided himself that he had established a sound and rational policy, the success of which depended not upon himself but on his successors[2]. But once again in Afghan affairs we have the lull before the storm. The fatal condition with regard to a British mission proved Lord Lytton's undoing. Yet once more in pursuance of our desire to make Afghanistan nominally a strong, united and independent kingdom, but in reality a puppet state, we had set up a ruler without authority, indeed one who was even less to be trusted than Shah Shuja. Yakub was as weak and unpopular as the last of the Durani monarchs, and his weakness and unpopularity

---

[1] *Afghan Blue Book* (5), 1881, *passim*.

[2] Balfour, *Lord Lytton's Indian Administration*, p. 335.

brought about their inevitable result. On Sept. 3rd Cavagnari, now the head of the British mission, and his suite were massacred. Only the day before he had sent a telegram to the Governor-General declaring "All's well," which bears a melancholy resemblance to a sentence in Sir William Mac-Naghten's last despatch, "The land is quiet, from Dan to Beersheba." How far Yakub Khan was implicated in the murder was never exactly determined, but it is most likely that the finding of the British Court appointed to examine the circumstances was the correct one. The conclusion to which this came was that Yakub did not instigate the massacre, but that he was not unwilling to take any advantage that might be obtainable from it, and did nothing to prevent the mutinous troops, who were directly responsible for it, from gratifying their fanaticism to the full. He probably thought the death of Cavagnari and his companions a convenient solution of his difficulties, in that owing to it he had got rid of a mission which he hated just as much as his father had done, although he had not dared to shew it. The British Government would content itself with punishing the mutineers and murderers, and would then withdraw and leave him to reign in peace.

The blow to Lord Lytton was a very severe one. His structure had fallen to pieces, and he

had to begin his building afresh. He now felt that
the time had come for putting his second plan into
action and for the disintegration of a treacherous
and troublesome kingdom. The conquest of Afghanistan was of course the first thing, but that
once accomplished Kabul must be separated from
Kandahar, never again to be united with it. Herat
with part of Sistan might be handed over to
Persia[1]. The policy of disintegrating Afghanistan
has already been discussed, but not this last recommendation, which was a counsel of despair. That
a country which had undergone none of the trials of
the campaign should reap all the fruits was manifestly absurd, especially as we had more reason to
dread the growing influence of Russia in Persia
than in Afghanistan, there being fewer opportunities
of combating it in the one case than in the other.
British influence in Persia had, except for short
intervals, been steadily decreasing throughout the
whole of the century, and to a far greater extent
in Northern Persia, to which both the Russian
dominions and Herat were adjacent, than in the
south. To hand over Herat to Persia as the result
of a war with Afghanistan would have been a complete stultification of all British efforts in Afghanistan. Herat was admitted by Lord Lytton to be
the key to India. It was quite as much the key to

[1] *Afghan Blue Book* (1), 1881, p. 6.

India when Afghanistan was strong and united as when it was weak and disintegrated, and if its possession meant anything at all to the British Empire in India, its maintenance in the hands of a friendly power over which Great Britain possessed some definite influence was an absolute necessity. Lord Lytton must have realized as much himself, as little more was heard of this part of his plans.

The Treaty of Gandamak makes a very definite stage in the second Afghan war, and that phase of the war which followed it bore an entirely different character from that which preceded. Lord Lytton had at last an absolutely righteous excuse for war. A treaty which definitely accepted a British mission, and gave guarantees for its safety, had been broken by the massacre of that mission, and war was therefore necessary to avenge the honour and maintain the prestige of the British nation. The first step was to occupy Kabul. All else might wait, but that must be done at once. No one realized that more fully than did Yakub Khan himself, as is shewn by his futile attempts to delay the advance upon his capital. He had hoped to be allowed to deal with the mutineers himself with the aid of, but with no unnecessary interference from, the British Government, but when he found that that was not to be the case and that the British were coming to look after their own interests, he gave matters up as hopeless

and added still further to the British difficulties by
taking refuge in Sir Frederick Roberts's camp on
Sept. 27th.   Kabul was occupied on October 12th,
but Yakub Khan had utilised the fortnight which
had elapsed since his arrival in the British lines, in
intriguing against the General to whom he had fled
for refuge.   Whilst clearing himself from all complicity in the murder of Cavagnari and his comrades,
he still hoped to rule once more in Kabul, free from
the overpowering shadow of the British presence.
But his dreams were rudely dispelled by the arrest
of his father-in-law Yahija Khan and certain other
unruly Afghans, who had done their best to make
the occupation of Kabul by the British as difficult
and dangerous as possible.   This measure convinced
Yakub that the British possessed a great deal too
much information concerning his recent actions,
and he felt that further rule in Afghanistan was
impossible   and   thereupon   spontaneously   abdi-
cated.

His abdication was welcomed by the Indian
Government as likely to assist it in carrying out
the most important parts of its policy.   For the
present the future of Kabul or of the Oxus
provinces could not be decided.   But Kandahar
was to be finally separated from Kabul, and Herat
might be handed over to Persia.   Retribution was
to be exacted from Kabul, and with a view to this
Lord Lytton proposed the imposition of a fine

upon its inhabitants and the demolition of the
Bala Hissar or some other prominent building
as a permanent mark of the punishment inflicted,
in addition to the execution of all who might be
discovered to have taken part in the recent outrage[1].
Eighty-seven persons found guilty of complicity in
Cavagnari's murder were executed, but the fine
threatened in Sir Frederick Roberts's proclamation
was never levied, nor were the buildings demolished.
Wiser than in 1842 the British in 1880 left no ruined
bazaar as a lasting memorial of their vengeance,
for a monument of British vengeance would also
be a monument to Afghan defeat, and it was therefore perhaps as well that the British did nothing to
augment the ill-will towards them already possessed
by the Afghans.

Yakub Khan was deported to India on Dec. 1st,
and throughout the winter Roberts, in spite of many
tribal risings, occupied Kabul, finding the fortifications Shere Ali had erected, when he began to fear
trouble with the British, of the greatest service.
Lord Lytton hoped to evacuate Afghanistan in the
early spring. If it were decided not to annex Kabul
and a suitable ruler were discovered for it, its importance was to be diminished as much as possible.
Shere Ali Khan, a descendant of the old Durani
kings, was to hold Kandahar subject to British
influence, new frontier railways were to be con-

[1] Roberts, *Forty-one Years in India*, p. 412.

structed, and the frontier tribes reduced to sub-
mission once for all. Shere Ali Khan was installed
at Kandahar in April, but no suitable candidate for
the throne of Kabul was then forthcoming, and its
evacuation had to be postponed to the autumn at
the latest, the Governor-General intending to give
arms and money to any claimant to it who appeared
likely to be successful. Had this policy been
carried out Northern Afghanistan would have been
left masterless and unsettled, but an unexpected
solution of the difficulties appeared in the person
of Abdur Rahman, Shere Ali's nephew, who had at
last been allowed by Russia to try his fortunes in
Afghanistan, as the opportunity offered by Yakub
Khan's departure was too favourable to be lost.
Kauffman, fully aware of the British difficulties and
of their willingness to accept any strong candidate for the throne of Kabul, probably thought
that, by sending forth Abdur Rahman, he was
welding a useful instrument for future use. In this
he was wofully mistaken. With the arrival of
Abdur Rahman upon the scene the second Afghan
war was virtually ended. Its wisdom has been fully
discussed in this chapter, and the conclusions need
not be here recapitulated. Lord Lytton was however to redeem to some extent his shattered reputation, before he handed over the reins of office to
a successor pledged to the reverse of the course of
action on which he himself had embarked.

CHAPTER V.

ABDUR RAHMAN KHAN, 1880—1901.

Correspondence between Lord Lytton and Abdur Rahman.—Change
of Government in England.—Lord Lytton succeeded by Lord
Ripon.—Evacuation of Kabul by the British.—Abdication of
Shere Ali, Wali of Kandahar.—The Kandahar controversy.—
Restoration of Kandahar to Abdur Rahman.—Defeat of Ayub
Khan by Abdur Rahman.—Character of the new Amir.—The
Afghan Boundary question.—Fall of Merv.—Appointment of a
Boundary Commission.—The Panjdeh incident.—The Amir's
conduct with regard to it.—Change of Government in England.
—Completion of the work of the Boundary Commission.—
The Rawal Pindi Durbar.—Further Boundary questions.—The
Indian Frontier Tribes.—The Pamirs.—The Durand Mission.
—The last Boundary Commission.—Trouble on the Frontier.
—Chitral. — Gilgit. — Frontier policy since 1899. — The new
Frontier Province.—Death of Abdur Rahman.

In pursuance of a desire to find some pleasant
aspects in Lord Lytton's Afghan policy, there has
been perhaps a tendency to praise him too highly
for his selection of Abdur Rahman as Governor of
Kabul. But opinions upon the point have been
by no means unanimous, and three hypotheses
have been advanced to account for it. Either
Lord Lytton was endowed with extraordinary

political foresight or he met with extraordinary good fortune. The remaining view is that he wished to reduce the theory of a buffer state to an absurdity[1]. The truth, as usual, probably lies midway between these theories. The last is the least possible, though it must be admitted that the Afghanistan, to which Lord Lytton intended Abdur Rahman to succeed, was to be a mere shadow of that ruled over by his predecessor, and that Kabul was to be shorn of much of its former glory. Further, Lord Lytton was extremely anxious to evacuate Afghanistan before the meeting of Parliament. The Afghan question was a party one, and Lord Beaconsfield's policy in that direction had been subjected to scathing criticism. It was therefore very desirable that the government of Afghanistan should be settled as early as possible, and this fact would have told in favour of a much less suitable candidate than Abdur Rahman, who was, as Lord Lytton wrote to Lord Cranbrook, a "ram caught in the thicket." But even after making these allowances some measure of credit is due to the Governor-General, who perhaps had formed a shrewder estimate of Abdur Rahman's character than had the Russians, and remembering the energy and ability he had displayed during the short and troublous reigns of

[1] Forbes, *Afghan Wars*, p. 206.

his father and uncle, knew that Afghanistan would
find in him a strong and wise ruler. Abdur Rahman
was in every way the candidate most entitled to the
throne of Kabul, but even now difficulties were by
no means at an end, and at one period it looked as
if, after all, the British Government would have to
seek a ruler for Kabul elsewhere.

The Governor-General was authorised to support Abdur Rahman on March 15th, 1880[1]. In a
letter to his mother the latter declared that he had
no intention of opposing the British Government,
and of this Sir Lepel Griffin, then in political
charge of Afghanistan, was made aware. Fortified
by this knowledge, he addressed a letter to Abdur
Rahman on April 1st, asking the Sirdar to make
what representations he might desire with regard
to his object in entering Afghanistan. The letter
was answered on April 15th by Abdur Rahman,
who declared that his hopes and wishes were
that, as long as Great Britain and Russia existed,
Afghanistan might remain quietly in ease and
peace, and "we hope of your friendship that,
sympathising with the people of Afghanistan, you
will place them under the honourable protection
of the two powers[2]." The latter request it was
of course impossible to grant. It may have been

---

[1] *Afghan Blue Book* (1), 1881, p. 9.
[2] *Ibid.*, p. 41.

made in accordance with Russian advice, for whilst
Abdur Rahman as yet owed nothing to Great
Britain, he was undoubtedly under some obligation
to the state which had pensioned him for eleven
years.   This obligation he was not inclined at
present to underrate, for whilst he was much more
sensible of the exact amount of the debt he owed
to Russia than were the British, it suited his immediate purpose to make it appear much larger than
it really was.   By so doing he foresaw that he
would be enabled to obtain much better terms
than might be the case if he appeared to close too
readily with Lord Lytton's offers.

Before Abdur Rahman's letter could be answered
a change of ministry had taken place in England.
On April 28th Mr Gladstone again became Prime
Minister, whilst the Marquis of Hartington succeeded Lord Cranbrook as Secretary of State for
India.   The new Government came into office
pledged to reverse in most respects the foreign
policy of its predecessor.   Of that Lord Lytton's
Afghan policy formed no unimportant part and he
therefore felt bound to resign office with the rest of
his party.   For the present, of course, the negotiations between Sir Lepel Griffin and Abdur Rahman
went on in accordance with instructions given by
him.

On April 15th Abdur Rahman was informed

that the British Government wished to withdraw
from Kabul as soon as it had established a friendly
Amir there, and he was consequently urged to
come to Kabul without delay. Whilst his sentiments towards Russia were appreciated, he was
told that no difficulty would arise in that direction,
as the British Government desired nothing different
from that which had already been agreed upon
between the two powers[1]. Abdur Rahman acknowledged this letter very cordially but shewed
no undue eagerness to come to Kabul, and through
the mission which conveyed his reply to Sir Lepel
Griffin desired information as to the exact extent
of his dominions, with special reference to Herat,
whether a British force or European envoy would
remain in Kabul, what enemy of the British
Government he was expected to repel, what
benefits the British Government proposed to
confer and what it expected in return[2].

This letter was answered in accordance with
instructions received from the new Governor-
General, the Marquis of Ripon, for by this time
Lord Lytton's resignation had taken effect and his
successor had arrived. Sir Lepel Griffin's reply to
Abdur Rahman on June 14th is therefore of great
importance in two connexions, in that it was a

[1] *Afghan Blue Book* (1), 1881, p. 46.
[2] *Abdur Rahman Khan's Autobiography*, I. 193.

manifesto of the policy the Marquis of Ripon at
this date intended to pursue with regard to Afghanistan, and also because it is the only document
which sets forth the formal relations between Great
Britain and Afghanistan which exist at the present
time. The treaties of 1855 and 1857 had been
superseded by that of Gandamak, which in turn
lapsed owing to Yakub Khan's abdication. The
letter of June 14th marks the foundation of the new
régime, and with its necessary complement, Abdur
Rahman's answer, still binds Afghanistan to Great
Britain. It has since been invested with much of
the significance of a treaty, and has, as we shall
see, been practically renewed by different Governor-
Generals on several subsequent occasions.

In it Abdur Rahman was assured that, as
Russia and Persia had promised to abstain from
all interference in Afghanistan, the ruler of Kabul
could have no relations with any power other than
Great Britain, and if any power attempted to interfere and such interference led to unprovoked
aggression, the British Government would assist
him in repelling it, provided he followed the advice
of that Government with reference to his external
relations. The British Government intended to
keep all that it had acquired by the Treaty of
Gandamak, and had definitely placed Kandahar
under a separate ruler. Herat—at this moment in

the possession of Ayub Khan, Shere Ali's second
son and the popular hero of Afghanistan—Abdur
Rahman might recover if he could. He was not
required to admit a British resident anywhere in
his dominions, though it might be desirable to
station a Mahomedan agent at Kabul[1].

Previous to the receipt of this letter Abdur
Rahman had been suspected of stirring up a jehad
against the British. There was probably some
foundation for the charge, his object being to
shew the British the extent of his influence in
Afghanistan and the advantages of coming to
terms with him. The desirability of breaking off
negotiations with him was discussed, and Sir
Frederick Roberts was somewhat unfairly blamed
for Yakub Khan's deportation to India, which
prevented his being put forward as a rival to
Abdur Rahman. Lord Ripon, however, saw the
reason for Abdur Rahman's actions, and he was
in consequence told by Sir Lepel Griffin, at the end
of the letter just mentioned, to intimate plainly
and at once his acceptance or refusal of the British
terms. The reply was prompt, for on June 22nd
he accepted them, but said nothing about Kandahar[2]. He was not in a position to complain
openly, but he felt its separation keenly, and never

[1] *Afghan Blue Book* (1), 1881, p. 47.
[2] *Ibid.*, p. 49.

regarded himself as the real ruler of Afghanistan until it had been restored to him again[1]. To Shere Ali Khan, the ruler of Kandahar, who had, he considered, done him an injury with the Russians, he bore no good will[2].

Abdur Rahman was informed on July 2nd that it was absolutely necessary that he should betake himself to Kabul at once and that he must, as far as possible, allay the distrust felt by the tribes towards the British. He still delayed, declaring that he must first go to Kohistan, but, as the country seemed quite quiet, it was determined that his public recognition should be no longer postponed and he was proclaimed Amir at a Durbar held on July 22nd[3]. This may have been the object for which he was waiting, for the meeting between himself and Sir Lepel Griffin took place very soon afterwards—on July 31st—and within a short time Kabul was evacuated, the last troops leaving it on Sept. 7th. The defeat of a British brigade at Maiwand was not allowed to interfere with the withdrawal of the British forces, but it furnished the first occasion for Abdur Rahman to display his loyalty towards the British, and Sir Frederick Roberts's wonderful march from

---

[1] *Abdur Rahman's Autobiography*, I. 195, 208.
[2] *Afghan Blue Book* (1) 1881, p. 49.
[3] *Ibid.*, p. 45.

Kabul to Kandahar owed much of its success to the new Amir's vigorous and tactful handling of the tribes which lined the route.

The disaster at Maiwand and the investment of Kandahar gave Lord Ripon's Government an unlooked for but most welcome opportunity for reversing its predecessor's policy with respect to that city. Shere Ali Khan, the ruler Lord Lytton had set up, had not proved a success, and it had rapidly become evident that he was not able to stand alone, and that, if he were to remain Wali of Kandahar, it could only be by the assistance of British troops. Shere Ali was by no means a strong ruler, he was disliked by the people of Kandahar, and was unable to make any head against the vigorous and energetic Ayub Khan. In addition, until Kandahar was restored to Afghanistan, Abdur Rahman had always a grievance against the British. Apart from the great importance from a military point of view which he attached to its possession, he had a sentimental feeling of affection for it as the cradle of his race[1].

Shere Ali ended his discomforts by resigning at the end of September and leaving Kandahar in December. A storm of controversy now broke out as to what should be done with the city. It is

[1] *Abdur Rahman's Autobiography*, I. 208.

impossible for anyone but an expert to pass any judgment upon the military questions of a controversy, the leaders of the opposite sides of which were Sir Frederick Roberts, supported by Sir Frederick Haines, and Lord Wolseley. The former advocated retention, the latter evacuation. How far the military authorities were influenced by political considerations it is impossible to say, but on the political side of the question there is much to be said for both parties.

The British Government had given solemn pledges to Shere Ali and his descendants that they should reign over Kandahar. Abdur Rahman had been informed more than once, even by Lord Ripon's Government, that Southern Afghanistan would never under any circumstances be restored to him, and to give him that district within a few months of such a definite statement looked very much like weakness. Again, although Quetta was at this time occupied, its occupation was looked upon in many quarters as merely temporary. By keeping Kandahar the British Government was pledging itself irrevocably to the retention of Quetta, as the one place was useless without the other. Finally by giving Kandahar to Abdur Rahman, Great Britain was making that ruler much too strong, and probably creating a rod for her own back in the future.

On the other hand it was argued that all
pledges to Shere Ali were conditional on his
being able to rule the province which had been
given him. To this task he had shewn himself
unequal and his resignation had been spontaneous.
The prestige of Great Britain might perhaps suffer
from the evacuation of Kandahar, but too much
might be sacrificed for a name and the end
might be mistaken for the means. Whilst we kept
Kandahar, we could never regard Abdur Rahman
as thoroughly well disposed towards us. In our
possession he would always regard it as a menace
and would intrigue to create disaffection there
towards British rule. By restoring it to him the
accession to his strength would not be so great
as was commonly supposed, as the people of
Kandahar differed somewhat in race from their
more northern brethren, and were by no means
well affected towards them, and in addition there
was always danger to be apprehended from Ayub
Khan. But above all we had established Abdur
Rahman at Kabul and a ruler of such undoubted
ability was bound to make himself strong with or
without Kandahar. There would therefore be in
any case a strong and united Afghanistan. It
remained to make it friendly and this could only
be done by giving Abdur Rahman Kandahar[1].

[1] *Later Afghan Blue Books* of 1881, *passim*.

The arguments for the evacuation of Kandahar won the day with a Government desirous in every way for retrenchment and for retirement within the borders of the India of 1878. In pursuance of their policy all British troops were withdrawn from Kandahar, and at the beginning of 1881 it was handed over to Abdur Rahman. That astute statesman did not appear at all eager to receive the possession which he had once declared he so highly prized. He pleaded with considerable truth that he was afraid of an attack upon Kandahar by his cousin Ayub, the victor of Maiwand, but his hesitation was also part of his settled policy of never appearing anxious to receive what he was sure to obtain in the end. By that means the value of the gift would be enhanced. And it was so in this case; for he was granted arms and ammunition together with a considerable sum of money to pay the expenses incurred in taking over his new acquisition[1]. At the same time the Kuram Valley was handed over to the independent government of the Turi tribe[2], and thus Quetta with the surrounding districts remained the only visible asset of the second Afghan war, and even Quetta, the more important part, had been acquired before the war commenced. The value of this however

---

[1] *Afghan Blue Book* (5), 1881, pp. 92 and 97.
[2] *Afghan Blue Book* (1), 1881, p. 95.

became more and more apparent as time went on, and all agitation for its evacuation completely died away.

Abdur Rahman had still many obstacles to overcome before he could be regarded as firmly seated upon the throne of Kabul, and indeed yet again in 1881 there seemed a strong possibility that the policy of a united Afghanistan would be a failure after all, and the country would once more be delivered over to anarchy. For, as Abdur Rahman had himself predicted, Ayub Khan made an attack upon Kandahar, which he succeeded in capturing. The Amir led an army from Kabul against him, but as he had since his accession done little or nothing to enhance his military reputation it was expected that he would be defeated. Fortunately, both for himself and Great Britain, this was not the case. Aided in great measure by the treachery so often apparent when Afghan armies meet each other, the Amir gained a decisive victory and Ayub fled back to Herat, only to find that, in his absence, it had been taken by Kudus Khan, Abdur Rahman's general[1]. He was thereupon compelled to retire to Persia, and Abdur Rahman was at last in possession of the whole of Afghanistan. His first step was to seal up all communication with India and to shew those, with

[1] *Abdur Rahman's Autobiography*, I. 215.

whose assistance during his recent struggles he was dissatisfied, that their country had at last found a master. He firmly believed that he had reached his high eminence through Divine assistance, as many times he had been encouraged to persevere by Divine revelation in dreams. It is not surprising that a deeply religious mind such as his should have held fast to this belief, for the untutored Oriental has not yet attained the stage of development of his Western brethren, and has not yet begun to doubt whether further revelation in this manner is possible. Aided by such a conviction and by his own natural ability it is scarcely surprising that Abdur Rahman proved a strong ruler. His career bears a certain resemblance to that of his grandfather Dost Mahomed, whom he greatly admired, and whom he regarded in many ways as his model. Allowed by the British to return to Afghanistan from exile, after the failure to protect a British mission on the part of the weak and untrustworthy rulers whom they had set up, each ruled his country well and wisely for twenty-one years. Both Dost Mahomed and Abdur Rahman were strong men and were never in any serious danger from aspirants to the throne. Abdur Rahman, though a greater man and more successful in enforcing order than Dost Mahomed, was not quite such an attractive character. To his

subjects he was an object of fear quite as much as
of veneration, and certainly no ruler in history was
so completely successful in devising punishments,
ingenious and fitting, but almost always just. But it
was his spy system, as complete and thorough as that
of the Inquisition in the palmy days of Spain, which
made him most detested. Abdur Rahman is not,
however, to be judged by Western standards and
probably much of what the British counted to him
for righteousness he regarded as his greatest faults.

Throughout the whole of his reign he endeavoured, in spite of a good deal of misunderstanding,
to keep loyally to his engagements with the Indian
Government, and relations with Afghanistan improved greatly. The first half of it may be
described as a period of comparative quiescence
in Afghan politics, the next seven years as a
period of comparative disturbance, to be succeeded
by another four years of peace and amity. Internally and externally the Amir's rule conferred great
benefits upon Afghanistan; internally, by giving it
unity and good government; externally, by giving
it a fixed and definite boundary both towards the
Russian and Indian Empires. The Russian boundary was the first to be demarcated. The time
had come for something quite different from the
nebulous Granville-Gortschakoff agreement, which,
unsatisfactory as it was when the Russian frontier

was some distance from that of Afghanistan, became
still more so when the two frontiers marched side
by side.   Accounts of the proceedings which resulted in the First Afghan Boundary Commission
differ considerably.   The Amir's version is somewhat highly coloured, probably with a view to
increase his prestige both in the eyes of his subjects
and of the British public.   The first three years of
his reign he had spent in making his throne secure.
So successful had he been in this that he now had
time to turn his attention to external relations.   He
says himself that he now considered it necessary to
mark out and delimit the boundaries of his relations
with foreign powers.   He had declared his intention
of being friendly with Great Britain, in the first
place, because he had made an agreement with that
country, and in the second, because it suited him
and his interests better.   Russia was much annoyed
with him on this account, and this annoyance was
to be increased, as the years went on, by the fact
that the Afghan Government had the courage to
put an end to Russian aggression by marking out
its boundary line.   Russia would also have preferred
that Afghanistan and Russia should divide the
frontier territory without the interference of Great
Britain, and she did not relish the closer approach
to that power implied by the visit to Rawal Pindi[1].

[1] *Abdur Rahman's Autobiography*, I. 241.

In reality the Amir had very little to do with the demarcation of his boundary, which was mainly the result of negotiations between Great Britain and Russia. Russia had been approached by Great Britain on the subject of Afghanistan in 1880, with the result that Lord Granville was assured that Kauffman had been forbidden to communicate with Abdur Rahman. In 1883 M. de Giers, the Russian Ambassador in London, informed the British Government that the Governor of Turkestan had been forbidden to transmit to the Amir letters of ceremony in favour of travellers. This was most satisfactory as far as it went, in that it made certain that there would be no repetition of the correspondence which had led Shere Ali on to his ruin, though it had been quite harmless at the outset.

The obligations contained in Sir Lepel Griffin's letter to the Amir were virtually renewed in 1883 by Lord Ripon's Government, and the Amir was bound more closely to British interests by the offer and acceptance of a subsidy of twelve lakhs of rupees yearly. This offer was made in view of the Russian advance, but the subsidy has been continued until the present time, and has, in fact, been considerably increased. Its wisdom has often been questioned, and it has been maintained that it is absurd to pay the Amir such a large sum of money whilst we have no British resident at Kabul, and consequently no guarantee that the money will be spent for the purpose for which it is given, namely in strengthening Afghanistan against a possible Russian invasion. But once the theory of a strong and independent Afghanistan is admitted, the money is after all but a small amount to pay for the protection of India against foreign invasion, and is a great deal more wisely spent than have been many of Great Britain's subsidies to Continental powers in the past. And, small as the sum is compared with the great object for which it is paid, it means very much to the usually impecunious ruler of Afghanistan, and is quite large enough to make him hesitate a long time before deciding to break faith with Great Britain.

In 1884 Merv fell before the Russian advance, as had Khiva and Samarcand. An expedition, with the nominal object of punishing the raids of the Turkoman Tekkes and other unruly tribes of Central Asia, had resulted in the permanent occupation of the city. This contingency the British Government had been dreading for many years, as it had quite a false idea of the importance of Merv with respect to India, and regarded it almost as another Herat. The greatness of Merv lies entirely in the past, and like many other celebrated Asiatic towns it has fallen from its former high estate. From a military point of view it has very little value, and Russia could seize Herat, not because it possesses Merv, but because it possesses Sarakhs and Panjdeh, towns which were no part of its dominions in 1884[1]. The occupation of Merv had however one important result. It gave Russia the commerce of Bokhara and Ferghana, two of the most fertile districts in Central Asia, and brought the armies of Trans-Caspia and Turkestan into connexion with each other[2].

At last there was a more than usually tangible result of the Russian advance. In consequence the British public was aroused to a fury of excitement and the Government was impelled to take action. In order to allay the growing distrust of the British nation at large the British and Russian Governments felt that the demarcation of a boundary between Afghanistan and the Russian Empire in Asia was absolutely necessary. In reality the proposal for a joint boundary commission emanated from Russia, but it was readily accepted by the British Government, which appointed Sir Peter Lumsden as the head of its section of the Commission. The Commission was a distinct step in the right direction, but had it taken place two

[1] Curzon, *Russia in Central Asia*, pp. 107, 121.
[2] Holdich, *The Indian Border-land*, p. 94.

years earlier the Amir would have got a much
better boundary.

The meeting of the Commissioners took place on
the North-West border of Afghanistan in October,
1884. The boundary to be settled was that between
the Hari Rudd and the Oxus. Russia had not failed
to lay hands in advance on all the territory she
could, and had occupied Pul-i-Khatun and Sarakhs.
The work of the Commission went on but slowly at
first, and seemed likely at one time to be broken
off altogether owing to the unfortunate collision at
Panjdeh, about which so much has been written.
The Amir would not appear to be very far wrong
when he ascribes most of the blame for that incident to the Liberal Government then in power in
England, which had placed the British Commissioners in a decidedly awkward position. They
had been despatched before a clear understanding
with Russia had been arrived at, and consequently,
whilst they were endeavouring to settle a boundary
line in Afghanistan, negotiations between Great
Britain and Russia on the subject were still proceeding in London. Lessar, a Russian agent, was
conducting a campaign in England, and was endeavouring to force the hands of the British Government by suggesting new boundary lines. Lord
Granville proposed an intermediate boundary, which
was declined, and three days later the Afghans and

Russians met in conflict at Panjdeh. The Amir
blamed the British Commissioners, with Sir Peter
Lumsden at their head, very severely for their
conduct on that occasion, and declared that by
refusing to assist the Afghans and by their ig-
nominious flight towards Herat, they had seriously
damaged British prestige in Afghanistan[1]. But it
is very difficult to see what else the unfortunate
British officers could have done, unless they desired
to provoke an immediate conflict between Great
Britain and Russia. The Afghans had been warned
that the responsibility for any further advance rested
on their own shoulders, and that, if they made it,
they could expect no help from the British. There
is no doubt that the Panjdeh incident might have
been avoided, but the blame for it, so far as the
British are concerned, does not lie upon the Commission but upon the Home Government which
had placed it in such an equivocal position. Had
the Commission been able to take up its position
at Panjdeh at the outset and to announce that it
was ready to commence the work of demarcation,
no untoward incident could have happened. But
the Home Government, which had contented itself
with feeble remonstrances in the preceding December at the Russian occupation of Pul-i-Khatun,
which undoubtedly by the Granville-Gortschakoff

[1] *Abdur Rahman's Autobiography*, I. 245.

agreement belonged to Abdur Rahman, was busy
negotiating over the heads of the Commission and
the result was Panjdeh. The British public, which
was firmly convinced that Panjdeh belonged to the
Amir, clamoured for war, but, fortunately for us,
the Amir, who perhaps knew more what war
between Great Britain and Russia meant than a
public which had forgotten the Crimea, declined
to stand upon his strict rights and war was thus
averted. The Amir's declaration that he was not
quite sure whether Panjdeh did in reality belong
to him, that he was indifferent as to its possession
because he could not trust the Sarik Turkomans,
and that he should be content with Zulfikars instead
of it, was probably partly due to the fact that he
was at this time at Rawal Pindi under the influence
of Lord Dufferin. His ties of friendship with Great
Britain had been greatly strengthened by his visit,
and he had no desire to shew his gratitude by pro-
moting what must inevitably be a very serious
struggle. He had, however, other reasons. A wise
and astute ruler, he was never anxious to incur
fresh or unnecessary responsibilities in the wild
and inhospitable regions of North-Western Afghanistan[1]. His desire for increased territory
always lay in the direction of the northern and
Eastern parts of his dominions. The Amir's

[1] Holdich, *The Indian Border-land*, p. 136.

action relaxed the tension and enabled the crisis
to be tided over. The change of Government
which took place in England in the autumn gave
a new strength to the Commission, which was
enabled to proceed with its work. Sir Peter
Lumsden, whose recall soon after Panjdeh aroused
considerable excitement in England, and was
regarded by a large section of English public
opinion as a prelude to a complete surrender to
Russian demands, was succeeded by Sir West
Ridgeway; the Russian political opposition col-
lapsed, as it so often does when a bold front is
presented to it, and by November, 1885, an arrangement with Russia had been arrived at. The
work of the Commission now proceeded smoothly
until the Amir himself added fresh complications.
Whether in consequence of a suspicion that the
British had ulterior motives in their lengthy stay
in his territories, a misconception of a second
mission under Lockhart, which consisted merely
of carriers, or sheer bad temper brought about
by an attack of gout with which he was prostrated
at the time, he became restless and wished the
mission withdrawn. It had however practically
finished its work and so the British section retired
to India by way of Kabul, where it was much
impressed by the great advance made since the
Amir's accession. The remaining negotiations were

completed by the Home Governments and the protocol was finally signed on July 22nd, 1887. The Amir declared himself quite satisfied with the boundary therein agreed upon, and expressed his high opinion of Sir West Ridgeway. The results of the Afghan Boundary Commission have great bearing on the future of all the three nations who participated in it. By it Afghanistan has not only been given a boundary by which, as Sir West Ridgeway declared, the Amir did not lose a penny of revenue, a single subject, or an acre of land which was occupied or cultivated by any Afghan subject, but a boundary which definitely limits the progress of Russia towards India. That boundary has been respected up to the present. The possibility of its violation is one of the problems of the future. The Commission had not completed the work of demarcation right up to the Pamirs and the possession of some small districts in this region was to be settled later.

The work of the Afghan Boundary Commission has been reviewed as a whole, but whilst it was in progress, a most important meeting, of which incidental mention has already been made, took place in the spring of 1885 at Rawal Pindi between the Amir and the Earl (afterwards Marquis) of Dufferin, Lord Ripon's successor in the Governor-Generalship. Somewhat uneasy because of the uncertain nature of his relations with Russia, to whom, as he says, he did not feel bound to sell his nation to shew his gratitude[1], the Amir desired still further confirmation of Sir Lepel Griffin's letter. The promises contained in it had already been renewed by the Marquis of Ripon, and the Amir had been given a yearly subsidy, but he was, nevertheless, extremely anxious for a meeting with the Governor-General. The result was the Great Durbar at Rawal Pindi, which was an unqualified success. Lord Dufferin seems to have exercised much the same kind of influence over Abdur Rahman as Lord Mayo had over Shere Ali, and throughout the whole of his Governor-Generalship there were never any difficulties with Afghanistan. The Amir was greatly pleased with his reception and quite satisfied with an assurance which Lord Granville had made early in 1885, that the policy of Great Britain towards Afghanistan included agreements with the Amir binding the British Government to regard as a hostile act any aggression upon his territory, of which Herat was a salient point. The heavy battery, arms and money with which Lord Dufferin presented him increased his satisfaction, whilst his private interviews with the Governor-General greatly strengthened his friendship towards Great Britain, and he was convinced that, in case of

[1] *Abdur Rahman's Autobiography*, II. 152.

Russian aggression, he might look to that country for aid without losing his independence. The practical outcome of these interviews was his speech at the Great Durbar of April 8th, 1885, when he declared,

" In return for this kindness and favour, I am ready with my arms and people to render any services that may be required of me or of the Afghan nation. As the British Government has declared that it will assist me in repelling any foreign enemy, so it is right and proper that Afghanistan should unite in the firmest manner and stand side by side with the British Government."

The Amir's loyalty to England was never in reality seriously shaken, but the good understanding brought about by Lord Dufferin did not remain intact under his successor, the Marquis of Lansdowne, who became Governor-General in 1888. Sir Frederick Roberts was now Commander-in-Chief in India and, as such, felt it his duty to increase the fortifications of the North-West frontier and to subjugate the frontier tribes. For the next ten years this policy brought about a great deal of unrest on the frontier, an unrest which the Amir was suspected of fomenting. Regarding himself as the head of the Sunnite branch of the Mahomedan religion in Central

Asia, he looked with suspicion upon the attempts of the British Government to bring the unruly frontier tribes under its influence. Whilst the Afghan boundary on the Russian side had been practically settled by the Commission of 1887, towards India it still remained in a most unsatisfactory state. Between the Indian frontier as settled in 1881 and Afghanistan proper there dwelt a number of fierce and barbarous Mahomedan tribes, owning allegiance to neither side, but acknowledging, in a very indefinite manner and much as suited their own purpose, the claims to religious supremacy put forward by the ruler of Kabul. The Amir was therefore in the habit of regarding these tribes as his subjects and much mistrusted British interference with them. The Afghan army, always greatly in excess of the resources of the country, badly disciplined and badly paid, had at this time very little to do. The Amir, who was desirous for obvious reasons of keeping it employed, thought this a favourable opportunity of attaining something more than a shadowy religious overlordship over the frontier tribes, and began to make attacks upon their independence. In consequence his relations with Great Britain became somewhat strained, and he therefore besought a confidential mission on this and other subjects in 1888. His request was granted, and Sir Mortimer

Durand was chosen as head of the proposed mission, which had however to be postponed owing to the rebellion of Ishak Khan, the Amir's cousin and Governor of Afghan Turkestan. Ishak Khan was speedily defeated, but the question had lapsed for a time to be revived again in 1892. There were many frontier questions to be settled with respect to both India and Russia. The Boundary Commission had not demarcated the frontier right up to the Pamirs and consequently there was a collision between the Afghans and Russians in that quarter in 1892. Shignan and Roshan, two small districts, were claimed by the Amir in consequence of the agreement of 1873, which made the Oxus the boundary between his dominions and those of Russia. The dispute really hinged upon the exact interpretation of that agreement, which left undecided which was the main stream of the Oxus. The Amir regarded himself as rightfully entitled to the territory in question, but declared that in any case he had a claim to it, as the Amir of Bokhara had occupied land on the left bank of the Oxus, and he was therefore justified in occupying land on the right[1]. Towards India, again, the Indian Government had annexed the Zhob district and opened up the Gomul Pass, a measure which had offended the

[1] *Abdur Rahman's Autobiography*, II. 153.

Amir almost as much as the Sistan boundary award had Shere Ali. The construction of the railway to New Chaman he looked upon as a menace to his independence, thinking it only a matter of time before the British Government would demand its extension to Kandahar, a policy which he knew had Sir Frederick Roberts's approval.

The situation in 1890 was for a time quite critical. Guns which the Amir had imported were stopped at Karachi and the tension was great. According to the Amir war was only averted by his personal appeal to Lord Salisbury, who, how-ever, he goes on to add, informed him that all difficulties must be settled with the officials of the Indian Government[1]. In reality neither side had any desire for a third Afghan war, and as an alternative method of settling difficulties the idea of a mission was again revived in 1892. Sir Frederick (now Lord) Roberts was to be its head but the choice was not a fortunate one. The Amir disliked Lord Roberts and Lord Lansdowne about equally. The Governor-General had had upon him much the same effect as Lord North-brook upon Shere Ali, and he resented his dictatorial tone in matters in which he thought the Government of India had no right to interfere.

[1] *Abdur Rahman's Autobiography*, II. 138.

Lord Roberts he admired as a soldier but looked upon as the incarnation of the forward policy on the frontier, which he so much detested, and he also was well aware that Lord Roberts had been the most persistent advocate for the retention of Kandahar in 1881. In addition he mistrusted the large military force which was to form the escort of the Commander-in-Chief. He therefore determined to delay the advent of a mission until after the departure of Lord Roberts from India, which he knew was approaching. His nominal excuse was the rebellion of the Hazara tribes in 1891 and 1892. This, the most serious of his many small wars, undoubtedly gave him a great deal of trouble, and he might have had still more difficulty in suppressing it had it not been for the fact that the Hazaras, an unruly tribe which held a strong position in the centre of his dominions, were members of the Shiah branch of the Mahomedan faith whilst the rest of Afghanistan is of the Sunnite profession. Nevertheless the Amir prided himself on the skill with which he utilised the rebellion and a serious illness, from which he was suffering at the time, as excuses to avoid the reception of Lord Roberts[1]. After the Commander-in-Chief had left India Abdur Rahman readily acquiesced in the visit to Kabul of Sir Mortimer

---

[1] *Abdur Rahman's Autobiography*, I. 282, II. 137, 157.

Durand, which took place towards the end of 1893.
That a British commissioner could visit the Afghan
capital in perfect safety shews the great advance
which had taken place under the Amir's rule and
is a hopeful sign for the future. All the points in
dispute were settled, though not perhaps altogether
to the Amir's satisfaction. He was very desirous
that the independent frontier tribes should be
acknowledged as coming within his sphere of influence. In reality they gave him but little trouble,
their attentions being mainly directed to the Indian
side of the frontier, which formed a much more
profitable hunting-ground for booty. And as the
head of his own branch of the Mahomedan faith
he foresaw great possibilities with regard to them
in the event of a struggle with India at any time.
He offered to make them loyal subjects to himself
and friendly to the British if their country were
added to his dominions. His petition was not
granted, but he was bribed to acquiesce in the
demarcation of the Indian frontier by the increase of his subsidy to eighteen lakhs of rupees
yearly. The negotiations between the Amir and
Sir Mortimer Durand were conducted in private
and no detailed account of them has ever been
made public, but the definite results arrived at
were that boundary lines both in the Pamirs and
on the Indian frontier were to be demarcated as

soon as possible. The dispute in Roshan and
Shignan was to be settled by the Amir receiving
the territory on his own bank of the Oxus, whilst
that on the right bank was to go to Russia, or
rather Bokhara. In addition to the increased
subsidy, the Amir was to receive arms and war
material from the Indian Government, and to be
allowed to import everything in the way of military
stores he might wish[1]. The question of an Afghan
envoy at the British Court was probably discussed
and the Amir was invited to visit England as
soon as he conveniently could. He accepted the
invitation and intended to come to England in
the summer after the conclusion of the mission.
Unfortunately he fell seriously ill and his place
was taken by his second son, Sirdar Nasrullah
Khan, who proved a most inefficient substitute
and whose visit was a complete failure. Had the
Amir come to England in person his visit would
have still further increased his friendship for the
British, and his chances of obtaining what he so
much desired—as we shall see by no means un-
reasonably—an Afghan envoy at the British Court,
would have been much increased.

The year 1895 saw the last of the boundary
commissions. That in the Pamirs shewed once
for all the utter impracticability of an invasion of

[1] *Abdur Rahman's Autobiography*, II. 162.

India from the extreme north. A long narrow
strip of Afghan territory separates the independent
tribes which we regard as within our sphere of
influence from Russia, which would have insurmountable difficulties in attacking India from this
direction. The second commission demarcated
the Indo-Afghan frontier in accordance with the
Durand agreement, but the result was not altogether satisfactory and the unrest which had
been prevalent along the frontier for some years
previously was little, if at all, diminished. The
independence of the tribes was practically left
untouched and this they did not at first realize.
They are beginning to understand that the fact
that they are within the British sphere of influence
does not necessarily mean that they are subject to
British rule and to treat the Durand boundary
as non-existent. The situation had, and still has,
additional disadvantages. The Amir administers
the country right up to his own boundary, but on
the other side of it are tribes whose independence
we have promised to respect whilst at the same
time we are nominally responsible to the Afghan
Government for their misdeeds. The responsibility
is one which we could not carry out if we would,
and the result has been that the Amir, quite aware
of this fact, has allowed his subjects to take the
law into their own hands and indulge in private

war with the frontier tribes[1].   In consequence there
have been some very troublesome years on the
frontier and some severe struggles, notably with
the Afridis and in the Chitral country.   Chitral,
in which country the Amir certainly interfered in
1894[2], has been definitely occupied and a frontier
agency re-established at Gilgit[3] (1893).   From a
military point of view the occupation of Chitral is
useless as there is no fear of a Russian invasion of
India from that direction.   Politically it may have
its uses as a means of establishing British influence
in those remote regions, and of educating the
frontier tribes, but it is questionable whether it is
in any case worth the expense and whether the
opening up of the country would not be of almost
as great advantage to Russia as to Great Britain.
The occupation of Chitral was, however, only part
of the forward policy of the last decade of the
nineteenth century of which the Afridi war of 1897
was the most notable outcome.   Such years as
1897 were very little to be desired for India, and
with the advent of Lord Curzon as Governor-
General in 1899 other and perhaps wiser counsels
prevailed.   For the first time since Lord Lawrence,
India had a Governor-General who was an expert

[1] *Times*, 1901 (Nov.).

[2] Holdich, *The Indian Border-land*, Chapter XI.

[3] The first was established by Lord Lytton.

in the politics of the Far East. In consequence
many vexed frontier questions have been settled
without any expenditure of blood and treasure.
New methods of dealing with the frontier tribes
have been adopted, methods much less calculated
to arouse the Amir's suspicion. Lord Lytton's
dream of a separate frontier province has at last
become a reality. In the future, frontier politics
will be under the direct supervision of the
Governor-General, and will be considered, as
indeed they should be, as a matter for the Indian
Empire as a whole and not as one for the Government of the Punjab alone. The policy adopted
towards the frontier tribes since 1899 has ceased
to be one of aggression, and they have been shewn
by more pacific measures that they are completely
dependent on British India for supplies, and in consequence are beginning to realize that acquiescence
in British rule will mean peace and prosperity.

The result of this policy was that the last
years of Abdur Rahman's reign were untroubled
by disputes with Great Britain. He had made
Lord Curzon's personal acquaintance at Kabul and
entertained a high opinion of his abilities[1]. He
therefore welcomed the new Governor-General's
accession to office.

Abdur Rahman Khan died in October, 1901.

---

[1] *Abdur Rahman's Autobiography*, II. 141.

He was not very old—not yet sixty, though the exact date of his birth would seem very uncertain—and might reasonably have looked forward to a longer term of life. With all his faults he was a very great ruler and possessed administrative genius of the highest order. Probably no other Afghan could have done so much for his country. In him England lost a good friend ; for, though his policy was to get all that he possibly could for Afghanistan and to increase its importance and his own in every way, for this he can hardly be blamed, and he recognized that Great Britain's objects were not altogether foreign to his own, and that he was much more likely to succeed by working harmoniously with that power than by endeavouring to play off Great Britain and Russia against each other. Friction was unavoidable at times. The state of Afghan civilization would alone account for that. But yet, during the twenty years of Abdur Rahman's reign, there can scarcely be said to have been a moment when the British Government regretted establishing him as ruler of Kabul or had any desire to reverse its policy towards Afghanistan.

CHAPTER VI.

THE FUTURE.

SOME apology might be deemed to be necessary
for the disproportion which has apparently been
observed in this essay in dealing with the past and
future relations of Afghanistan with Great Britain,
were it not for the fact that only after attentive
examination of the past history of those relations
can any deduction be drawn or forecast made as
to their possible trend in the future. Much has
been done in the past to solve the great question
of the future of Afghanistan. Its history in the
nineteenth century would seem to point clearly to
the conclusion that neither a policy of masterly
inactivity, such as that of Lords Mayo and North-

brook, nor one of aggression, such as that of Lords
Auckland and Lytton, is likely to meet with success.   The policy of a strong and united Afghanistan, independent but bound by the closest ties
of interest to the British, which possesses elements
of both the other policies but leans definitely to
neither, has been the most successful in the past
and will probably remain so in the future.

Having therefore determined at the outset with
all the British Governments of the last twenty years
that the maintenance of the *status quo* is, on the
whole, the best possible course both for India
and Afghanistan, we must now consider how long
that *status quo* can last, in what way it is likely to
be ended, and what modifications in it are necessary or advisable.   A year ago it might have been
confidently predicted that it would last some years,
namely, until Abdur Rahman's death, which at
that period appeared moderately remote.   A year
ago it was confidently predicted that the Amir's
death would be followed by anarchy in Afghanistan until one of his sons had killed or driven into
exile all the others.   Such was the logical conclusion to be drawn from the state of affairs at the
death of every Amir since the foundation of the
Afghan Empire.   But in this as in other things
the Afghanistan of Abdur Rahman shewed a
great improvement on that of his predecessors.

Habibullah Khan, the late Amir's eldest son,
whom by many acts in his lifetime he had
marked out as his heir and of whose ability he
had a high opinion, succeeded peacefully to his
father's throne and was accepted without hesitation
by his brothers.   He was also formally acknowledged by the British Government, towards which
he declared he intended to maintain the policy of
his father.   He was in turn assured that so long as
he did so his father's subsidy would be continued.
Russia also recognized him as his father's heir.   But
there are, at the time of writing[1], rumours of unrest
in Afghanistan.   The Afghan is proverbially a hiber-
nating animal.   In a country of climatic extremes
rebellion is a luxury in which there is no desire for
indulgence in the winter months, and therefore the
summer is always chosen for military operations.
It is therefore possible that the prophets of anarchy
will after all be found correct, and that the summer
months will find Habibullah's difficulties by no
means over, but only just beginning.   But it is
hardly probable that Habibullah will meet with
the difficulties of his forefathers in establishing his
position.   He has undoubtedly greater abilities
than any other of his father's sons.   His capabili-
ties as Governor of Kabul were more than once
shewn during his father's lifetime to the late Amir's

[1] February, 1902.

entire satisfaction. He has, too, the arsenal and
the army at his back. Lastly, his recognition by
the British Government gives him a decided start
of the other competitors for the throne. It is by
no means consonant with British interests that
there should be anarchy in Afghanistan. Of this
both he and his rivals are probably well aware, and
the knowledge will make for peace. For in the
event of a struggle in Afghanistan the British
Government would assist Habibullah with arms,
ammunition, and money, though not with troops.

There has never been any lack of pretenders to
the throne of Kabul, and at the present time they
are as numerous as ever. There is nothing to be
feared from the Suddozai dynasty, whose influence
in Afghanistan is absolutely extinct. Ishak Khan,
however, watches and waits at Samarcand as did
Abdur Rahman before him. But he lacks his
cousin's abilities both as a statesman and a soldier,
has little following in Afghanistan, and is not likely
to prove a thorn in Habibullah's side. Ayub Khan
and his brother Yakub, Shere Ali's sons, are in
India under British surveillance. The latter would
not return to Afghanistan if he could, the former
probably could not if he would. The Indian
Government would not, of its own free will, allow
him to add to complications in Afghanistan, and
has doubtless taken sufficient precautions to pre-

vent his escape. Long years of captivity and exile
must have sapped his energies and made him little
inclined to embark upon another career of adven-
ture. He is to this day a popular hero in Afghanistan, chiefly owing to the fact that at Maiwand
he inflicted upon the British troops one of the most
severe disasters they have ever suffered in Asia,
and also because of his daring seizure of Kandahar
in 1881. But it is most unlikely that he will ever
return to Afghanistan, and Habibullah has therefore nothing to fear from him. There remain then
two other of Abdur Rahman's sons, Nasrullah
Khan and Mahomed Umar Jan. Nasrullah may
be ruled out of the contest at once. His visit to
England shewed that he was a prince of little
capacity, and he is not likely to make any head
against the reigning Amir. He labours under the
additional disadvantage of being Abdur Rahman's
son by the same mother as Habibullah, and therefore in no case has any legitimate claims to the
throne. Habibullah's most dangerous rival is probably Mahomed Umar Jan, the son of the Queen-
Mother, a woman of ability and ambition. Abdur
Rahman himself maintained that none of his sons
had any claim to better birth than the others[1]. He
may have done this to increase his own prestige,
for the same question had arisen at Dost Maho-

[1] *Abdur Rahman's Autobiography,* II. 8.

med's death, and Shere Ali had been preferred to Abdur Rahman's father Afzal, the eldest son, as being of royal birth on both sides. But whatever Mahomed Omar's claims to royal descent he is very young and this fact will help Habibullah, as the Afghans have no desire to be ruled by a woman. Habibullah would seem at the present time to be engaged in conciliating the religious element in his dominions. The summons of the most prominent Afghan mullah to Kabul is certainly not a policy of which his father would have approved, but it is likely to assist him in any contest with his rivals.

The whole question of the policy to be pursued by the British Government in the case of pretenders to the throne of Kabul is as we have said a very difficult one and may mean much to Afghanistan in the future. The probabilities are that it will not arise at present, and perhaps if Habibullah reigns long enough some more definite principle of succession than has hitherto been the case may be adopted in Afghanistan. In the past the sons of the last Amir have fought the matter out amongst themselves, and affairs have often been still further complicated by the claims under Mohamedan law of brothers to the succession in preference to those of sons. The danger to the British Government lies in the fact that it may find itself

in a false position owing to acknowledgment and
assistance rendered to a weak and incapable claimant.   Obviously its best course is to acknowledge
that claimant to the throne who, either by his own
abilities or the definite statements of the reigning
Amir, is marked out for the succession during the
lifetime of his father.   There will be less risk in
doing this, but in the possibility of anarchy at the
death of an Amir lies one of the greatest obstacles
to the continued independence of Afghanistan.

We may then regard the present state of affairs
as likely to last until Habibullah's death.   Meanwhile if Habibullah fulfils his early promise, and
shews himself desirous of continuing his father's
policy, it has been held that there are one or two
steps which might advantageously be taken to
increase his friendly feelings towards the British
Government.   He was doubtless well trained by
his father with regard to the policy to be pursued
by Afghanistan towards Great Britain and Russia.
The late Amir in his autobiography laid down
many precepts for the guidance of his successors.
One of their great aims, he stated more than once,
should be to secure the right to send representatives to the Courts of all the great powers, and
to receive their representatives at Kabul.   It
might, he fully acknowledged, be many years before this, in his opinion, most desirable state of

affairs could be brought about, and in the meantime his successors should direct all their energies
towards persuading the British Government to receive an Afghan envoy at the Court of St James,
as well as at that of the Governor-General. Had
he come to England this would have been his great
object, as it was that of his inefficient and tactless
substitute Nasrullah Khan. It is extremely doubtful whether in any case he would have been successful, but there are weighty reasons in favour of his
proposal which he could have laid before the British
Government with much more cogency than did
the incapable Nasrullah. The defence of the Indian
Empire has ceased to be a local matter and has
long since become one for Imperial concern. India
is certainly the most important and perhaps the
most valuable of the British possessions, and therefore its safety is a consideration of vital importance
to the whole Empire and not to Indian statesmen
alone. An attack upon it may be made by Russia,
not because of any advance or disturbances in
Afghanistan, but in furtherance of designs in China,
Corea, or Constantinople. It is, in consequence,
very important that a view other than that of
Indian statesmen, who do not always possess the
experience or the wide views of the present Governor-General, should be in evidence. This would
be furnished by an Afghan envoy in London, who

would represent to the British Government aspects
of the question of Indian frontier defence which do
not always appeal to the Indian. The increased
work given the Foreign Office would be infinitesi-
mal in comparison with the satisfaction accruing
to Afghanistan and the value of the information
received. It is in the last degree improbable that
the British Government will ever allow Afghanistan
to be represented at foreign Courts or foreign Courts
to have ambassadors at Kabul. Abdur Rahman
always fully admitted that the foreign relations of
his country were entirely under the control of the
British Government and were likely to remain so.
In consequence his hope that Afghanistan would
one day be admitted into the comity of nations on
equal terms was little better than an idle dream.
But Afghanistan might be granted an envoy in
London. As a natural result, what Lord Lytton
desired so much—a British representative at Kabul
—would follow. The Amir's request for the one
would imply that he would allow the other. Of
Abdur Rahman's ability to protect a British mission there was, at any rate during the latter years
of his reign, not the slightest doubt. Much as
he restricted the presence of foreigners in his
dominions, he could, when he chose, guarantee
that Englishmen could travel from end to end of
them in perfect safety. Of this the passage of the

Boundary Commissions through Afghanistan, the visit of Sir Mortimer Durand to Kabul, and the residence in that city of English in the Amir's service, are sufficient evidence. But the character and aims of the new Amir have yet to shew themselves, and it remains to be seen whether the political ideals his father cherished will recommend themselves to him. Certainly no British agent should be sent to Kabul until he requests either that or its equivalent, an envoy in London. Assuming, however, that Habibullah will follow in this matter the instructions left for his guidance by his father, the objections to the continued payment of his subsidy would be completely answered. For the presence of an Afghan representative in London and of a British representative at Kabul would be in itself a guarantee that the subsidy would be spent on the object Great Britain has so much at heart, the strengthening of Afghanistan against a Russian invasion. The idea that Russia would also demand an agent at the Court of Kabul may be dismissed as chimerical. No British Government could listen to any such request for a moment, since Afghanistan is as entirely within the British sphere of influence as is Bokhara within that of Russia. Great Britain could at any rate readily retort by demanding a representative at the Court of Bokhara.

The arguments in favour of an Afghan representative in London have been stated at some length
as the matter was one very near to the heart of the
late Amir. He did not perhaps fully realize the
great difficulties which might prevent the British
Government granting his request. The experience
of that Government itself in the matter of double
representation is not such as to admit of its encouragement of such a departure in diplomacy on
the part of Afghanistan. Early in the last century
missions were sent to Persia, both from England
and from India, in order to enlist the aid of that
country against any schemes of French invasion.
The result was an unseemly wrangle with regard
to precedence and other matters which disgusted
the Shah and prevented the achievement of any
useful object. Were Afghanistan to have a representative in London a similar state of affairs might
quite conceivably arise. For the presence of an
Afghan envoy in London, even if it did not neces-
sitate that of one at Calcutta, might provoke an
unedifying competition between the Foreign and
India Offices. The relations of Afghanistan with
the British Empire, though of interest to the Empire as a whole, are of paramount importance to
India alone, as is recognized in the fact that the
Amir's subsidy is paid from the Indian and not from
the Imperial exchequer. As long as this is the

case the Indian Government must have a control-
ling voice over Afghan foreign policy. It has even
been suggested in this connexion by competent
statesmen that even though Persia receives no
subsidy either from Great Britain or from India, it
would be a great advantage were her relations
with Great Britain conducted through the Government of Calcutta, which, if for no other reason
than that of closer proximity, is capable of treating
them in a more intelligent manner than the Home
Government.

Argue against it as he might, by accepting
a subsidy Abdur Rahman placed himself in an
inferior position. It is quite true that in the past
foreign powers have received subsidies from Great
Britain without thereby losing their right to have
an embassy at the British Court or in any way
abrogating their control over their own foreign
policy. But such subsidies have been paid in consequence of a definite treaty of alliance and in
pursuance of some temporary object in time of war.
With the conclusion of peace the subsidy has come
to an end. The case is different with regard to
Afghanistan. The subsidy is annual, is paid in
time of peace, and in consequence of no treaty of
alliance. This fact renders the Amir a British
dependant. The British Government has neither
the intention nor the desire to interfere in the

internal affairs of Afghanistan, but so long as the Amir receives a subsidy from Calcutta he is a prince dependent upon India, and as such has no more claim to an envoy in London than any of the native Indian princes. Were the subsidy received from London the case might perhaps be different, but until it is the Indian Government is the only one with which the Amir is called upon to deal.

Further, the presence of an Afghan envoy in London might add greatly to the difficulties of the British Government in case of a disturbance of the political atmosphere. Afghanistan acts, as we have seen, as a protecting outwork to the most vulnerable part of a very important British possession. In the event of difficulties elsewhere it is therefore by no means improbable that an Afghan envoy in London would act as a centre of intrigue with regard to foreign powers not well affected towards Great Britain.

Whilst a recommendation of the continuation of the *status quo* must seem to many an unsatisfactory conclusion, the question which has just been discussed is not one, fortunately, in which it is either necessary or desirable that British statesmen should take the initiative, and they are not called upon to come to any decision with regard to it until Habibullah or one of his successors again raises it.

Abdur Rahman's other great dream for the benefit of his country, the acquisition of a port on the Arabian Sea, has also little prospect of realization.   But British statesmen should aim at some new and more equitable trade arrangements with Afghanistan by which the prohibitory Afghan tariffs might be removed.

Such is, in outline, the policy which would seem most desirable of pursuit towards Afghanistan so long as the present state of affairs continues.   But again we are faced with the problem, How long can it last ?   The causes most likely to bring about its downfall are a Russian violation of the Afghan frontier, with or without subsequent war with Great Britain, and anarchy in Afghanistan itself in consequence of the death or incapacity of the reigning Amir.   These may in reality be resolved into one, as the same constant factor, Russia, is present in each case.   It is therefore evident that the British Government should seize the first opportunity to exchange some more definite views with that power on the subject of Afghanistan, and should make the fact that it would regard any violation of the Afghan frontier as a *casus belli* clearly understood. By so doing much trouble may be avoided in the future.   But the desirable opportunity may not arise, and British statesmen cannot perhaps be expected to go out of their way to create it.

Again, they may not feel inclined to bind themselves to the hard and fast policy indicated in this
suggestion, and may prefer to deal with a Russian
advance as the occasion may demand. Hence it is
on the whole probable that the present somewhat
unsatisfactory state of our relations with Russia
with regard to Afghanistan will continue for many
years to come. Neutralization has often been suggested as the best possible solution of the Central
Asian difficulties, and Belgium and Switzerland are
instanced as examples of its success. But neutralization has never been a political expedient which
has recommended itself to the Oriental mind, or
proved practicable in dealing with Oriental states.
There are, too, other obstacles which prevent its
successful application to Afghanistan. Great Britain and Russia are alone concerned in the maintenance of Afghan independence, Great Britain to
a greater extent than Russia. To no other powers
in the world, except perhaps Persia, which is too
weak to have any voice in the matter, does its
continued existence as a separate state matter in
the least. All, or nearly all the great powers are
interested in the independence of Switzerland and
Belgium, and in that fact lies the peace and safety
of these two countries. That will never be the
case in Afghanistan. Even if it were neutralized,
a course manifestly unfair to Great Britain, con-

sidering the blood and treasure spent upon it by
that country, the position of the Amir would be
very far from pleasant. A barbarous state in the
situation of Afghanistan, between two great and
civilized Empires, is bound to gravitate one way or
the other, and, whilst neutralization would only
augment the effort of the two great powers to
obtain the ear of the ruler of Kabul in time of
peace, it would also, in all probability, be totally
disregarded in the event of an outbreak of war.

Neutralization then being impossible, the
eventualities we have just enumerated remain to
be considered. Taking the more probable—
anarchy in Afghanistan in consequence of the
death or incapability of the Amir—first, the
difficulty of the British Government would lie
in the attitude taken up by Russia. That
power might regard the occasion as a favourable one for making an advance, or might foment
the disturbances in other ways. Very possibly
there might be a legitimate excuse for such
an action, as a state of anarchy in Afghanistan
might mean a state of anarchy on both sides
of the frontier, in putting an end to which Russia
might be justified in using every means in her
power. The policy marked out for the British
Government in such a case would demand that
it should exert all its influence in endeavouring

to induce the Russian Government to abstain
from all interference. It should itself allow the
combatants to fight the matter out, not trying in
any way to force its own choice upon Afghanistan,
but aiding with money and war material the candidate with the best abilities and the best claims,
or if the two do not coincide, the candidate who is
the most likely to put an end to a state of affairs
which is not in the interests of either India or
Afghanistan. Matters will thus adjust themselves,
and the old policy may by this means be maintained.   But such a course of action may be
absolutely impossible owing to the dearth of a
suitable candidate, and a still more intricate
problem may present itself. The dismemberment
of Afghanistan might then become a necessity and
the only possible solution of difficulties.   Great
Britain and Russia alone are, as we have seen,
concerned in the independence of Afghanistan, and
its disintegration would therefore be the result of
a mutual agreement between those two powers.
The boundary between the two great Empires,
the "conterminous frontier," has been fixed by
nature in the mountains of the Hindu Kush,
which, ethnologically as well as physically, divide
Afghanistan into two well-marked portions.   The
northern provinces would go to Russia, the southern become incorporated in the Indian Empire.

This was one of Lord Lytton's schemes and may one day become an accomplished fact. The whole of Afghanistan would be of little use to India. Setting aside the vexed military question as to which side of a mountain range is the best for defensive purposes, the possession of the northern half of Afghanistan would be of no conceivable advantage to India as a protection against Russian invasion.

The provinces added to the Indian Empire as the result of this arrangement would not be the more fertile ones, but they are infinitely the more important from a military point of view. The different characters of the districts are reflected in those of their inhabitants. The Turkomans and Usbegs, who live to the north of the Hindu Kush, are very poor soldiers, whilst the Afghans and Ghilzais who inhabit Southern Afghanistan, led by British officers, would form some of the finest fighting material in the world[1]. The last twenty years may have witnessed some change in the Afghan sentiments towards Great Britain. Hated as overlords, the British might be welcomed as conquerors. For it has been held by many who know Afghanistan well that the late Amir's rule was oppressive in the extreme and very irksome to the majority of his subjects. The mild and equitable British rule

[1] Holdich, *The Indian Border-land*, p. 372.

might therefore be welcomed as a relief by all, except the nobles, parasites, and fanatics of the Afghan Court. Whether it would be acquiesced in after the memory of the tyrannical rule of the Barakzais, with its odious spy system, had died away is open to question. It is the nature of the Central Asian peoples to make a gallant and heroic struggle until they are hopelessly beaten, and then to submit in gloomy silence to the inevitable. This might be the case in Afghanistan, and the Afghans, influenced by the example of their Mahomedan brethren in India, might soon develop into loyal British subjects. One result of a struggle against the new order of things might however be the production of the Afghan leader for whom the British had hitherto been searching in vain.

Even admitting all the consequences which arise from the oppressive and irksome nature of the Amir's rule it may seriously be doubted whether the addition of the greater part of Afghanistan to the Indian Empire is to say the least desirable. It is impossible to speak hopefully of the resources of the country. Abdur Rahman, who did so much to develop them, and who was a very practical judge, was yet of the opinion that Afghanistan would prove a poor field for European enterprise for at least fifty years. A land, as Lord Wellesley contemptuously termed it, of rocks, sands, deserts, ice, and snow, the complete though rudimentary system of Afghan irrigation has done practically all that can be done for it, and its relation to the greater part of India could never, even under the most favourable circumstances, be other than that of Scotland to the remainder of Great Britain. Not more than one-tenth of it could possibly be brought under cultivation ; that it is very rich in mines has yet to be shewn, and even if it possesses mines, they could only be worked under great difficulties owing to the extremes of climate and hindrances to transport.   Railways it has none, and the Amir would view with great suspicion any request by the British Government for that extension of the Indian railway system to Kandahar, Jellalabad, and Kabul which Lord Roberts considered so necessary for the defence of the frontier.   There remains much to be done in the matter of political education in Afghanistan before this will be permitted.   From the point of view of trade, therefore, the addition of Afghanistan to India would help the latter but little, and from the military standpoint the enlargement would prove most expensive.   The present system of subsidising Afghanistan is cheap and would probably work well in the event of a Russian invasion.   If Afghanistan were added to India, and the frontiers

of the British and Russian Empires became conterminous, Great Britain in India would be still
more in the position of a Continental power than
it is to-day, and very great expenditure would have
to be incurred in fortifying the Indian Empire
against the prospect of attack from the North-
West. The Trans-Caspian railway is a factor in
Asiatic politics which cannot be neglected. However inefficient it may be at the present time—
and its defects have been somewhat overrated in
England[1]—it will be greatly improved as time
goes on and will always be a valuable military
asset to Russia in consolidating her vast possessions
and enabling her to mobilize troops easily on the
Afghan frontier in case of need. Another question
to be considered in this connexion is the junction
of the Indian and Russian railway systems. The
advantages of this step are by no means obvious,
though it has often been declared that it is only
a matter of time because it is necessary to the
advancement of civilization, and the private interests of two nations will not be allowed to
stand in the way where those of the whole world
are concerned. Commercially and politically the
benefits it would confer upon India would certainly
be small. Commercially, because of the merciless
prohibitory tariffs imposed by Russia, which would

---

[1] Curzon, *Russia in Central Asia*, p. 271.

most effectively kill all trade by this route ; politically, because it would be a source of great unrest. It would consolidate the Russian dominions right up to the gates of Kandahar, and by so doing would always give the British Empire in India a feeling of insecurity, in addition to lessening its prestige in Afghanistan. It is not therefore likely to commend itself to British statesmen, who have no desire to place such a powerful weapon in the hands of a possible adversary.

The possible effects upon Afghanistan of a Russian advance, with or without subsequent war with Great Britain, have now to be considered. We have given Afghanistan a frontier, and Russia has promised to respect that frontier. But at some future time when Great Britain has her hands full in another part of the world—whilst she is, for example, augmenting that Empire in Africa for which Asia has of late been somewhat neglected— Russia may seize Herat or some other important strategical point on the Afghan frontier. It has been said that the violation of the Afghan frontier by Russia would not lead to war, though war might, and probably would lead to the violation of that frontier[1]. In accordance with this theory Great Britain's proper course in answer to a Russian advance upon Afghanistan would be to

[1] Holdich, *The Indian Border-land*, p. 367.

seize Kandahar and Jellalabad. The Amir's kingdom would thereupon fall to pieces and the
conterminous frontier would, as before, be the
result.

But whilst such a course might seem to British
statesmen the most expedient, it would not be the
most honourable, and probably, in the end, not the
most profitable. Only in one most unlikely contingency could it be justified. If the Amir ceded
territory to Russia of his own free will, Great
Britain would have reasonable grounds for taking
possession of Kandahar and Jellalabad, but in no
other case. For the British Government is bound
by the most solemn pledges to protect Afghanistan
from all aggression, if that country follows its advice
with regard to its external relations. Therefore
any violation of Afghan territory by Russia should
be followed by a declaration of war in all parts of
the world with Great Britain, and the Amir should
be helped by every means in British power. We
have made him the most powerful Mahomedan
sovereign in the world, and Russia would find
Afghanistan assisted by Great Britain much more
than a match. It is perhaps extremely unlikely
that in the event of war between Great Britain
and Russia the whole Afghan people would range
itself on the same side. But Great Britain would
start with a great advantage, and would attract to

itself the best fighting material in Afghanistan, if she declared at the outset her intention of maintaining Afghan independence inviolate and of annexing no part of that kingdom. Abdur Rahman maintained that he could throw 100,000 men into Herat within a week. There was probably a great deal of truth in this statement and, at any rate, it may serve to remind both British and Russian statesmen that Afghanistan as a military power is by no means to be despised, and, especially at the commencement of a war, would prove a most troublesome enemy. It would therefore on the whole pay British statesmen much better in the end to assist Afghanistan in the recovery of its territory than to join in the struggle for increased dominion and increased responsibilities. The question is much complicated by the European element. A threat of war with Great Britain might make Russia withdraw at once, but it would be impossible for Great Britain to assist the Amir without at the same time committing herself to war everywhere else. Be that as it may, British honour demands that Afghanistan should be supported in every way in the event of unprovoked aggression.

Finally, we have to discuss the position of Afghanistan in reference to a Russian invasion of India brought about by a *casus belli* to be

found in Afghanistan itself or elsewhere. One of
our greatest difficulties in reference to Afghanistan
lies in the fact that we can advise the Amir but
cannot altogether control him. We stand in much
the same position with regard to Russia in respect
of him as we do with regard to Afghanistan in
respect of the frontier tribes. Every Amir should
therefore be given distinctly to understand—and
the warning cannot be too frequently repeated—
that he will receive no assistance if he undertakes
aggression on his own account, and that if he
shews any inclination to do so his subsidy will
be at once withdrawn. If this is done the danger
of Russia finding any pretext for war in Afghanistan itself will be minimised. The Amir's attitude
towards a Russian advance upon India in furtherance of Russian schemes elsewhere would, of course,
be all important. Russia would endeavour to obtain
his good will and might succeed in doing so. But,
as time goes on, it will become as patent to the
successive Amirs as it was to Abdur Rahman that
little is to be gained by assisting Russia in any
invasion of India. Quite apart from the fact that
in the event of a Russian defeat the British would
punish Afghanistan most thoroughly and completely for any assistance it might render the
invaders, there are very weighty reasons why
Afghanistan should oppose the Russians with all

its might. Russia could only hope to attain permanent possession of India after a terrific struggle with Great Britain and the hopeless deterioration of the British Empire. Such an end to the contest would also imply the loss of Great Britain's command of the sea. India is singularly open to attacks from the sea, and in addition one of its chief commercial assets, opium, necessitates an open sea passage to China. No Amir, with a particle of wisdom, could fail to observe that the permanent occupation of India by Russia would mean the end of Afghanistan. He might at the outset get the bribe promised for his assistance, Peshawar or some other district, but in the end Russia would allow no obstacle to free communication with all parts of her Empire and would not suffer a petty independent state to block her path. Afghanistan would follow India and the Amir's diplomacy would have been in vain.

Again, if Russia were to attack India with no hope of conquering it but only in order to distract Great Britain's attention, and to keep a large section of the British army occupied whilst she was moving elsewhere, the Amir would be in no better plight. For the Indian frontier on the North-West, though not impregnable, is yet extremely strong, and is capable of defence even by a weakened and deteriorated Empire for a very

long period. During this period Afghanistan
would be practically in the hands of Russia. It
can scarcely support its own population, still less
a great Russian army, and the attempt would
mean its ruin. The Afghans dislike the Russians personally much more than they do the
British, because of their intemperate and filthy
habits, and the contempt of the Mahomedan
religion they have shewn in Central Asia. However much an alliance with Russia might recommend itself to a foolish Amir it would probably
be much against the inclinations of the majority
of his people, and Afghanistan has a rough form
of constitutional government which might be found
useful in forcing the ruler's hands. Great Britain
is a very good paymaster, and in the event of a
conflict with Russia in Afghanistan would be in an
infinitely better position than her antagonist in the
matter of supplies. She could do much to help
the Afghans in this direction in addition to maintaining her own army.

Great Britain stands in a better position in
Afghanistan to-day than she has ever done. The
memory of the two useless Afghan wars is fading
away, whilst Russia has two quite recent blunders
against her credit, her refusal to assist Shere Ali
after luring him on, and her aggressive frontier
action as exemplified in the affairs of Pandjeh in

1885 and of the Pamirs in 1892. Abdur Rahman was not altogether pleased with Great Britain many times. He thought that his warnings were not regarded as seriously as they should have been, and the steps he deemed necessary to the safety of Afghanistan not taken until it was too late. But he recognized the wisdom of Great Britain's attempt to make his kingdom a strong bulwark against Russian aggression, and did his best to assist in it. It is the duty of British and Indian statesmen of the future to consolidate and increase in every possible way the good understanding between Great Britain in India and Afghanistan. The time may come when Afghanistan may share the fate of many another state and be blotted off the map of Asia. Until then it should be Great Britain's aim to follow out unhesitatingly the policy, which is being so ably pursued at present, and which is most consistent with British honour and with British interests, that of a strong, united, and friendly Afghanistan.

LIST OF AUTHORITIES.

Adye, Sir J.	Indian Frontier Policy	1897
Aitchison, Sir C.	Lord Lawrence	1892
Anon.	Causes of the Afghan War	1879
Balfour, Lady B.	Lord Lytton's Indian Administration	1900
Colquhoun, A. R.	Russia against India	1900
Curzon, Lord	Russia in Central Asia	1889
Forbes, A.	The Afghan Wars	1892
Frazer, R. W.	British India	1896
Hanna, Col. H. B.	The Second Afghan War, Vol. I.	1899
Holdich, Sir T. H.	The Indian Border Land	1901
Kaye, Sir J. W.	History of the War in Afghanistan	1851
Keene, H. G.	History of India	1893
Lumsden, Sir P. S.	Lumsden of the Guides	1899
Lyall, Sir A.	The Rise and Expansion of the British Dominion in India	1894
Malcolm, Sir John	History of India, 1784—1823	1826
Marshman, J. C.	History of India	1901
Roberts, Lord	Forty One Years in India	1900
Sultan Mahomed Khan	Life of Abdur Rahman	1900
Trotter, Capt. L. J.	History of India under Queen Victoria	1886
,, ,,	Earl of Auckland	1893
Wheeler, S.	The Ameer Abdur Rahman	1895
Yate, A. C.	England and Russia face to face in Asia	1887

For EU product safety concerns, contact us at Calle de José Abascal, 56–1°,
28003 Madrid, Spain or eugpsr@cambridge.org.

www.ingramcontent.com/pod-product-compliance
Ingram Content Group UK Ltd.
Pitfield, Milton Keynes, MK11 3LW, UK
UKHW012331130625
459647UK00009B/222